THE
FIRST AMERICANS

JAY WERTZ

ANDRE
DEUTSCH

AUTHOR'S ACKNOWLEDGEMENT

To Olga Newborg Wertz, mother and history teacher, who first influenced me to study and appreciate the past.

THIS IS A CARLTON BOOK

Design copyright © André Deutsch Limited 2018

Text copyright © First Person Productions Limited 2008, 2018

This edition published in 2018 by André Deutsch Limited
A division of the Carlton Publishing Group
20 Mortimer Street, London W1T 3JW

Printed in Dubai

A CIP catalogue for this book is available from the British Library

ISBN-13: 978-0-233-00578-2

Front cover photograph: Wolf Robe, by Frank Rinehart.
Back cover photographs: (Left) Three Cheyenne warriors, by Edward Curtis; (Right) Sitting Bull, by D. F. Barry.

THE
FIRST AMERICANS

JAY WERTZ

FOREWORD BY

DR. BLUE CLARK

ANDRE
DEUTSCH

Horses at White Clay Creek watering hole with a
Lakota Sioux tipi camp in the background, 1891.

CONTENTS

FOREWORD

∧∧∧∧∧

Native Americans have been a defining part of the United States' experience. Their presence helped to shape the American consciousness and character. Jay Wertz opens the Native American background of the United States to the general reader in a unique way. He has done a great service for the reader in making documents of history more accessible. His work enables the reader to hold copies of original documents and read the words that helped form events.

Historical acts leap off the page of the book's documents and Jay Wertz successfully places the documents in their historical context. The author surveys the panoramic sweep of U.S. Native American history from prehistory to the present. The variety of textual documentation reflects the complexity of the subject, with pull-out manuscript examples, boxed segments, narrative, photographs, maps, and more. His is an interactive approach on paper. His method takes the reader into the complex interactions that took place after the coming of Europeans to the continent. He includes international diplomacy, trade, settlement, treaty councils, land cessions, and assimilation policies. All of those activities and more resulted in opening the territory of the expanding United States to settlement and resource removal.

Native American history is messy. There were conflicts when cultures clashed. However, beyond Indian warfare, which dominated early literature and motion pictures, were many peaceful pursuits. Commerce, sharing, marriage, missions, and other interactions affected the relations between Native peoples and non-natives. I personally enjoyed viewing the documents within their contexts and believe families will be surprised at the fun and excitement they will experience in sharing their own exploration. Native American history is a rich tapestry and Jay Wertz provides the reader with a doorway into the full enjoyment of all of that richness.

Blue Clark (Muscogee/Creek)
David Pendleton Chair of American Indian Studies and Professor
Oklahoma City University
Oklahoma City, Oklahoma

INTRODUCTION

Native Americans. The term is the most descriptive of any used to characterize the subjects of this book. Whether they arrived exclusively over the land bridge connecting North America with Asia, a long held theory, or in combination with a variety of sea-based immigrations, as new research is suggesting, they are truly the original human inhabitants of the continent, and thereby warrant the use of the "native" identifier.

As one of the most stereotyped groups of people in history, Native Americans have endured a great amount of misunderstanding in the roughly 500 years since continuous contact with Europeans began. Far from being "savages," as they were labeled for centuries, Native Americans had a unique understanding of the land they inhabited and the creatures they shared the world with. Though technology wasn't necessarily at the forefront of their developing cultures, it had a place in them. Their spirituality, however, developed into a complex and extremely important part of their cultures.

The one thing Native Americans did not originally have was a written language, although pictorial communications were used and are discussed in this book. It is therefore, perhaps, unusual to create a history of Native Americans in a work that features documents. However, the power of this work is that documents can reveal not just the events, but also the dynamics of a great variety of subjects.

Contact with Europeans, and later, Euro-Americans, has been an integral part of Native American history for the last half millennium. Nothing in the lives of North American Indians has escaped the influence of whites, African Americans, and other immigrants that arrived later in the hemisphere. Therefore the treaties, maps, land grants, and declarations that reflect the interactions between Native Americans and other cultures are great aids to understanding the course of history. By the same token, Native Americans had wide ranging influence on later immigrants to the New World and their enormous impact on the political, economic, and social aspects of North America have continued through the centuries.

Through a combination of textual and visual elements, well-known and rarely seen, an illustrative canvas of many aspects of Native American history and life is offered in this book. It is my fervent hope that this work, influenced by much more expansive legacies, both written and oral, will serve as a conduit to further inspection and study of the rich heritage of the subjects of this book.

Jay Wertz
Los Angeles, California

IN THE BEGINNING: THE ICE AGE MIGRATION TO THE WESTERN HEMISPHERE

THE HUMAN PREOCCUPATION WITH "WHERE WE CAME FROM" IS A FASCINATION THAT CAN TAKE MANY FORMS. THESE RANGE FROM SIMPLY TRACING ONE'S FAMILY TREE, TO ADVANCED GENEALOGY, AND ALL THE WAY TO COMPLEX INTERDISCIPLINARY SCIENTIFIC STUDIES WHICH SEEK TO DEVELOP THEORIES AND ESTABLISH CONCLUSIONS ABOUT THE ORIGINS OF MANKIND.

OPPOSITE The mastodon and mammoth were different Ice Age species of pachyderm. This skeleton of an adult mastodon was discovered virtually intact in New York State. The artist's rendering of the Wooly Mammoth is based on evidence from paleontological discoveries.

FAR LEFT This biface, or "toolkit," was found in the Lake Manix archeological dig in California's Mojave Desert and is believed to be 14,500 years old. It is called a toolkit because the user would chip off a piece for cutting or scraping, discard the piece, and then repeat the process. When the toolkit was nearly gone, the core was shaped into a spear point.

ABOVE LEFT The *atlatl* or spear-thrower was the most common hunting weapon of Paleo-Indian man. It utilized a simple weight and fulcrum mechanical principle to increase the power of the thrower's forearm.

LEFT The skull of a saber-tooth cat. This carnivore of the Pleistocene Epoch competed for game with man in the late Ice Age.

It is no different for the peoples who have inhabited the western hemisphere for thousands of years, the Native Americans, and those who study them. Native American cultures typically hold family and spiritual roots in high regard, and as a consequence the study of their origins commands much attention.

The search for Native American origins is a dynamic and continuing process. For centuries, the theories of how man came to inhabit the western hemisphere were varied and sometimes fantastic. One such idea was that early man came from Europe in small boats, following the North Atlantic route later taken by the Vikings. Then, in the early twentieth century, chance discoveries combined with rapidly advancing scientific techniques indicated that humans followed other animals who traveled from northeast Asia, today's Siberia, on to the American continent during the Pleistocene epoch.

Around 50,000–8,000 years ago, during the great Ice Age—which actually saw a series of advances and retreats in the polar glaciers—the land mass of Beringia appeared and then disappeared in several cycles. It is often referred to as a bridge between Asia and Alaska. During this time there were several occasions when mankind could have followed large

THE ROLE OF ARCHEOLOGISTS

The study of prehistoric man relies on the work of many scientific disciplines. Without written records, much about Paleo-Indians must be inferred. The role of the archeologist is to discover, retrieve, and interpret physical evidence. The field office of the archeologist is the dig site, a term universally given to the location of objects and remains, whether on the surface, covered by earth and sediment or under water. The home office is the laboratory, where a number of identification techniques are employed. Archeologists combine their findings with the work of geologists, meteorologists, and others to draw conclusions about the objects and remains they discover.

ABOVE A modern artistic rendering of a Paleo-Indian hunting party stalking a herd of mammoths. In the background are long-horned bison. If a successful strike was made on a beast, the hunting party would follow the injured animal until it tired from loss of blood and fell dead.

animals across the land bridge, or alternatively moved eastward on watercraft.

The reason archeologists are able to determine the existence of these early humans, now referred to scientifically as Paleo-Indians, is because evidence such as the discovery of objects made by humans mixed with animal bones substantiates their existence in the New World. Paleontologists, examining fossilized remains of Pleistocene animals such as mammoths, mastodons, sloths, and saber-tooth tigers, made the first recorded discovery of a mixed find in Folsom, New Mexico, in 1926, thereby establishing the first key to dating the Paleo-Indian settlement. More discoveries were made in New Mexico, Colorado, Chile, Mexico, and elsewhere. New scientific techniques, especially Carbon-14

dating, which uses the radioactive decay of naturally occurring isotopes to indicate the age of organic material, confirmed the dates.

From this and other data, a unified theory was developed: that Paleo-Indians crossed Beringia from their previous homes in Siberia in search of big game—the food source that preceded them. They followed the ice-free path down the east face of the Rocky Mountains and settled in North America, or moved south into Mexico, Central, and South America. They operated singly or in small groups to trap, kill, and carve up their prey, using implements of stone, such as those that were discovered among animal bones at Folsom and elsewhere. The lack of human bones at these sites indicates they succeeded in their hunts without great danger from their prey or their

THE ROLE OF ANTHROPOLOGISTS

Anthropology deals exclusively with human culture. In the case of Paleo-Indian, there is too little evidence at the present time to indicate the existence of a complex social hierarchy, but that changed as pre-historic Native Americans moved through time. Early humans are referred to by the location where their existence was discovered, hence Folsom Man, for example. The anthropologist takes the findings of the archeologists and other scientists and forms culturally distinct patterns. Often the anthropologist works side by side with the archeologist at the dig site. The noted twentieth century anthropologist Lawrence Leaky worked at the Calico dig site in the Mojave Desert and his work helped give rise to Calico Man.

carnivorous animal competitors. Later human arrivals, who settled in Alaska and along the Arctic Circle, may have used boats to cross the strait about 7,000 years ago, as water was beginning to permanently cover Beringia. These peoples' prey was Pleistocene fish and sea mammals, indicating their familiarity with a maritime way of life.

But is this unified theory the end of the search for the origin of Native Americans? Undoubtedly not. As time passes, new discoveries and techniques reveal yet more questions to be answered. In California's great Mojave Desert stone artifacts discovered at a knapping station, or tool shop, have for several decades fueled speculation that the first presence of Paleo-Indians could be dated to more than 35,000 years ago. Other discoveries in Chile and the Appalachians challenge traditional thinking on the time and even the origin of other immigrations to the hemisphere. The combined efforts of scientists will continue to make new discoveries that support or modify current thinking on the subject.

LEFT These spear points are examples of Folsom or Clovis Points (named after two early archeological finds in New Mexico). The top point is fluted, meaning grooved, in the center to hold it more securely to a wooden spear.

ABOVE This is a skull of the forerunner of the modern horse. These animals were a food source for the Paleo-Indians, who never used the beasts for transportation or draught.

THE ABORIGINAL IMPRINT

THREE MILLENNIA OR SO BEFORE THE PRESENT TIME, PALEO-
INDIAN CULTURE WAS GRADUALLY EVOLVING. JUST AS THE SEARCH
FOR FOOD HAD PROPELLED MAN INTO THE NEW WORLD, SO FOOD
BECAME THE MAIN DRIVING FORCE BEHIND THE FORMATION OF
GROUPS AND CULTURES (WHICH ARE TODAY KNOWN AS TRIBES).

The large game animals of the Pleistocene epoch were being driven to extinction by ecological factors, such as the drying of the land. Wasteful hunting practices also hastened the extinction, a process which occurred later in the New World—where there were only rougly a million humans spread across two continents—than in the Old World. Although new breeds of animals emerged, the change made man place more attention on plant food sources.

The first method of exploiting flora for food was gathering, a relatively simple development, since an abundance of nutritional plant foods existed in most areas. Before long, agriculture, the deliberate cultivation of plants for food, became a part of life in the New World. These Meso-Indians (the successors to the Paleo-Indians) took to agriculture more readily in Mexico and farther south than in the north, probably for ecological reasons. The appearance of advanced city-states among the Incas, Mayans, and Aztecs depended primarily on the rise of agriculture, which freed their populations from the rigors of a transient lifestyle and allowed the establishment of permanent settlements and

ABOVE LEFT This mask dated to 1700 B.C., is attributed to the Dorset culture, the first Eskimo aboriginal culture, named after Cape Dorset, Alaska, where artifacts from the culture were found. The Dorset Eskimos spread eastward to Newfoundland and the west coast of Greenland, starting in about 3000 B.C.

LEFT Stone tools of early Native Americans. Shown here are a cutting tool (left) and a spear point from Saskatchewan, Canada (right).

more complex cultures. The Calusa tribe of Florida, as a large organized community not dependent on agriculture, was a notable exception.

The change also came to Meso-Indians of North America, but more gradually. As reliance on agriculture increased, virtually all the forming cultures of the western hemisphere came to share two distinct traits: a preoccupation with death; and a sense that a higher natural authority controlled the fate of their crops. Care for the dead and worship of—and sometimes sacrifice to—the gods were central features of their cultures, traits which even today Native Americans recognize as an important part of their heritage. Discoveries relating to this phase of development about 3000 B.C. have revealed much about the beliefs and lifestyles of these people. Agricultural tools of the period and new implements of food preparation and storage discovered alongside the points and knives of hunting indicate evolution of lifestyles. More complex cultural themes began to appear. For example, the Adena People and their eventual successors, the Hopewell People, were not only fine artisans of decorative pottery and adornment, they also gave great attention to the dead by building burial mounds. The huge effort in altering the terrain in this way indicated the importance of death and spiritual issues.

The term "people" rather than "man" is now used to refer to these societies because the evidence points to cultures and larger groups rather than an individual or single hunting party. Hence the Adena culture relates to discoveries made

NOTABLE NATIVE AMERICAN ARCHEOLOGICAL AREAS

Earliest Period of Findings
- ● Paleo-Indian
- ● Archaic
- ● Post-Archaic

EARLY POTTERY

The shift away from near exclusive reliance on big game for food led to the development of pottery and baskets, to gather, prepare, cook, and store their foodstuffs. Initially, wild seeds and grains were gathered, and later the three historic staples of the Native American diet: squash, beans, and maize (Indian corn) were grown. Many of these plant foods were prepared by grinding them into meal with the ancient equivalent of a mortar and pestle. Then the meal was liquefied and cooked in a pot or heated immersion style, by dropping hot stones into the vessel.

near that Ohio town. But the names of Native American cultures are also derived from other factors. The Old Copper People, for example, discovered and pounded the naturally occurring metal into shapes. The Red Paint People used a dye made from plants to adorn coffins with the life-inferring color of blood, a symbol of their preoccupation with death.

The Archaic Stage (late hunting/gathering to early agricultural) cultures engaged in trade, as evidenced by their use of raw materials in their artifacts whose natural source was often quite distant. Though few traders ventured long distances, it is likely that cultures traded with those nearby and articles and ideas passed from place to place one culture at a time. One notable exception was the passage of cultural ideas and items northward from the advanced cultures of Mexico. However, about 1,800 years ago, a new phase in the evolution of North American cultures began, a period of regression, a kind of

"Dark Ages," followed by a period of progressive social change.

By A.D. 700 a new influence spread northward through the Mississippi Valley. From this Mississippian culture, which incorporated pyramids and temples and a hierarchy of priests, the peoples of North America acquired more complex craft and architectural techniques, and a more developed spiritual life. Some scientists see an influence brought from Mexico, while others see the North American mounds, earthen, not stone, as locally developed. Finds in Louisiana dating from 3400 B.C. support the latter theory. The various groups were beginning to divide into tribes, though not necessarily on the basis of language, of which there were half a dozen main tongues and dozens of sub-dialects. All of these developments would continue for several hundred years until the greatest impact on Native American culture in history occurred—first contact with the white man.

ABOVE This jar in the shape of a standing human female figure was of the Mississippian culture. The pottery design has a non-symmetrical front and back as a human body does. It was discovered in Cross County, Arkansas.

ABOVE Stone tools of early Native Americans, top: an adze from the southeastern United States, bottom: a very large obsidian ceremonial blade from Ross County, Ohio.

ABOVE Snow goggles from A.D. 500. The early Eskimos of the Arctic region devised snow goggles like these to prevent snow blindness while traveling across the frozen ground.

RIGHT This bird effigy ornament from the Hopewell culture was cut from mica by a craftsman. The symmetrical design with one side mirroring the other was common.

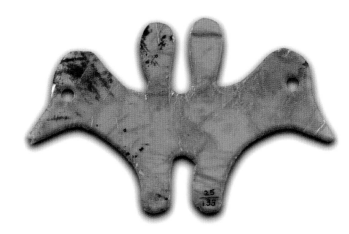

MOUND BUILDERS

Beginning with the Adena People (2000 B.C.–A.D. 200) a tradition of burial mounds wove its way into the culture of the North American peoples. Among the Hopewell People, the mounds took on greater size and advanced design. The Mississippian mounds, large man-made rectangular earthen plateaus topped by temples, are thought to be Mexican influenced. They required a community large enough to provide a workforce of builders, and a social command structure to attain the result. The largest of these mounds discovered is a 16-acre pyramid in the Mississippian city of Cahokia, now in Illinois, east of St. Louis. Cahokia which reached the height of its cultural importance around A.D. 1000–1100. Other burial mounds have been discovered in Georgia, Virginia, in Great Lakes glacial kames, and elsewhere.

EASTERN & WOODLAND NATIVE AMERICAN TRIBES

IN THE EASTERN PORTION OF NORTH AMERICA, AN AREA BOUNDED
ROUGHLY ON THE NORTH BY THE ST. LAWRENCE RIVER AND ON THE
WEST AND SOUTH BY THE LOWER OHIO AND MISSISSIPPI RIVERS,
THE PRIMORDIAL LANDSCAPE WAS COVERED BY DENSE FORESTS.

Here, the prehistoric inhabitants, moving eastward in a search for food and survival, found a different environment to that in the west of the continent. There was large game to be sure, but mastodons and other large game moved less easily through the dense forests and underbrush and were able to disappear more quickly. Here the descendants of the Red Paint People, the Adena-Hopewell, and other ancient groups began to establish a pattern of hunting, fishing, and gathering, and augmented foot travel with an early adaptation of water travel.

The first identifiable inhabitants of this region, in what are now eastern Canada and the northeastern and north central United States, were Algonquian speakers. From this common background, tribes developed in dissimilar ways. Some adapted quickly to farming the three staple crops of maize, squash, and beans. Others, in close proximity to the Atlantic Ocean and other bodies of water, derived most of their food from fishing and mollusk gathering. They made use of the abundant forests to gather wood for their fires, to build their homes and construct their watercraft.

Among these tribes were the Micmac, Penobscot, Massachuset, Narraganset, Pequot, Wappinger, Delaware,

LEFT Tee Yee Neen Ho Ga Row was considered an Iroquois emperor and was one of four Mohawk chiefs of Canada on a diplomatic mission to London in 1710. This lithograph is from a painting made during the visit by Jan Verelst.

HIAWATHA

Sometime in the sixteenth century a Huron prophet named Deganawidah was supposedly inspired through a dream to stop the infighting among the Iroquoian speakers. His prophet Hiawatha—a Mohawk according to the Indian legend that was later fictionalized with some variations by Henry Wadsworth Longfellow—paddled from tribe to tribe, spreading the message of peace and brotherhood. This resulted in the formation of the League of Iroquois Nations. The confederation was formed from the Cayuga, Seneca, Oneida, Mohawk, and Onondaga tribes, with the later inclusion of the Tuscarora. In reality, it may have been the new threat of the white man that caused the tribes to unite.

Nanticoke, and Powhatan. They hunted deer, beaver, rabbit, and game-birds with bow and arrow. Their use of native flint, quartz, and slate produced fine arrowheads and other tools. Many lived in longhouses constructed of elm bark which covered a base of lodge poles made of saplings. The culture had a strong, maternally influenced family base, and many families, with their beds and personal items stacked along the sides, occupied one longhouse. In a center corridor, cooking fires illuminated the interior and produced a great deal of smoke, despite the presence of exhaust cut-outs in the roof. A traditional cross-legged sitting position, which over the years has been attributed to Native Americans, had practical roots. It allowed the longhouse dwellers to conduct their affairs at a level which kept their faces underneath the lingering smoke.

The tribes who lived on the coast substituted smaller conical houses of bark, grouped in small villages, for the longhouses. They gathered clams, lobsters, and mussels from the shoreline and shallow lagoons and fished with nets. Their dugout canoes, adaptable to the interior rivers, were also used to navigate the rocky shorelines of the Atlantic. There was conflict between some tribes; those less adept at farming would raid the corn and squash stocks of their neighbors. A cluster of these Algonquian tribes built up a large empire (known as the Powhatan Confederacy), which in the sixteenth and seventeenth centuries stretched from the Chesapeake Bay to the coast of present-day North Carolina. All tribes, however, worshipped a higher authority in a nature-based spirit world where gods took the form of animal creatures, the same rabbit, deer, and elk which they hunted.

ABOVE A wooden dugout canoe, a typical vessel of an eastern tribe. It was discovered submerged on the coast of Connecticut.

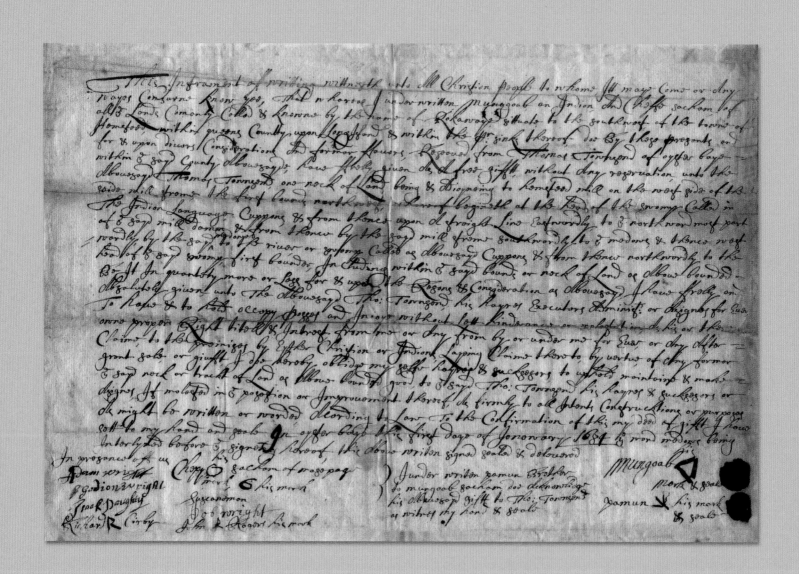

QUEENS CITY DEED

This deed to Queens City, New York, was created on 1 January 1684 and
was signed by Mungoab, an Indian chief, and English colonists. His mark
is in the lower right corner. As with Manhattan, a small quantity of gifts
were exchanged for a large tract of land. See Translations, page 156.

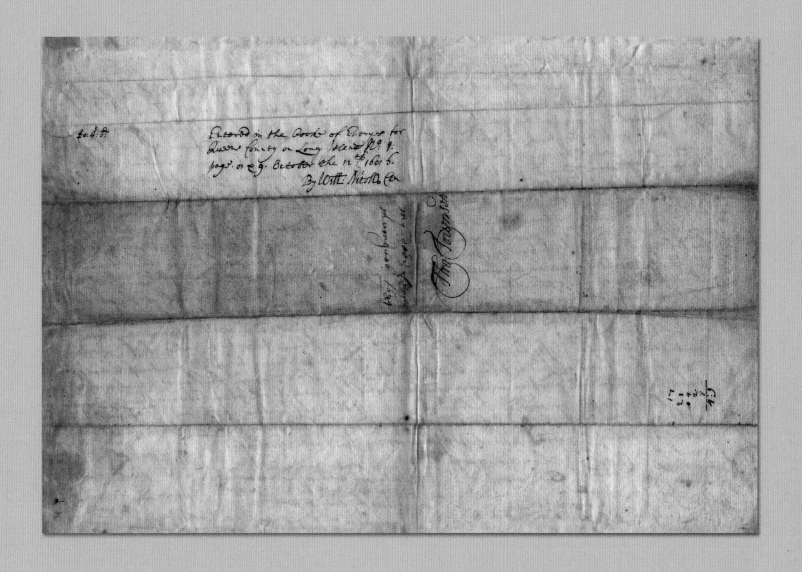

£0:4:8

Recorded in the Booke of Charges for
Queens County on Long Island No: 1:
page: 0229. October the 12th 1686.

By Wm: Nicolls Clr

Tho: Tongus

Into this Algonquian world another group of people whose origins are now believed to be in the primal forests of New York, began to expand their influence. These were the Iroquoian speakers who formed the Seneca, Mohawk, Oneida, Cayuga, and Onondaga tribes. They settled the interior of what are now northern Pennsylvania, eastern Ohio, and New York. They also lived in longhouses, traveled in birch-bark canoes, and were skilled hunters with the bow and arrow. A key difference among the Iroquois was the fact that the women owned the dwellings and land and appointed members of the male tribal council, a ruling force with democratic attributes. They sometimes traded and sometimes warred against their neighbors of the Delaware, Susquehanna, and other tribes, and eventually adopted the farming techniques of their neighbors. Another group of Algonquian speakers settled the Great Lakes region, gathering wild rice and eventually turning to farming. These were the Miami, Ottawa, Fox, Ojibwa, and other tribes, and a few Siouan speakers. The Eastern and Woodland tribes settled into a peaceful coexistence, even as a great confederation, the five nations of

LEFT This 1703 price list of goods sold to Indians uses a measure of beaver pelts, when in season, to compute the cost of European goods and measure the value of other animal skins. For example, two yards of cotton could be had for one beaver pelt. Incredibly, it took eight mink pelts to equal the value of one beaver skin.

WAMPUM

Wampum, the Native American form of diplomatic credential and currency, had its origins among the coastal tribes of the east. It gained widespread acceptance among tribes and with European traders as a measure of value and friendship. It was made from small seashells of varying colors that were laboriously ground and shaped to a spherical design, then bored out and strung on tiny cords of sinew. The color, patterns, and designs of the wampum bands had accepted common values. Although much is made of the cheating of Native Americans by the white settlers who traded beads for land, in fact the labor saved in using European glass beads to make wampum strings did give the beads much added value.

Iroquois, gave that group immense power in the region. But the balance was interrupted with the coming of European explorers and settlers beginning in the seventeenth century.

TOP This birch-bark bucket of the Penobscot tribe was made from one piece of bark cut to size and sealed with pine tar. The tribes of Maine and eastern Canada made a number of useful containers from bark.

ABOVE The wooden ball-headed club was a weapon commonly used by eastern and central Woodland tribes in raids and sometimes open combat and preceded the tomahawk. This Munsee Delaware example was found in southwestern Ontario.

RIGHT Black Beaver, born in 1808, was an influential member of the Delaware (Lenape) tribe who traveled throughout North America. The story of the Delaware (the name is completely European in origin) tribe is a sad one. Battled into submission by the Iroquois Confederacy and swindled in land dealings with colonists, they were also one of the tribes hardest hit by European diseases.

FAR RIGHT The unhappy looking woman in this lithograph is Sarah Slocum, who was kidnapped and raised by the Lenape sometime in the seventeenth century. European captives were sometimes ransomed back to their people. Others adapted to tribal life.

ABOVE Dwellings of the Woodland tribes of the Great Lakes region. Shown here are a conical bison-skin lodge and an oblong birch-bark lodge.

BLAEU MAP 1635

Dutchman Willem Janszoon Blaeu, 1571–1638, created this map of the New World in 1635. It is unusual in that the west cardinal point is at the top of the map. New Netherlands, New England and Virginia are identified and some features, such as Long Island, are quite accurately portrayed. Note the illustrations of Indians in canoes in the Atlantic Ocean.

The title lists "Nova Belgica" but the area claimed by the Netherlands is listed as Niev Nederlandt as well as Novum Belgium (in Latin), reflecting some subtle differences in what explorers were calling the newly discovered areas. The pictorial map has a lot of accurate details including the communities of Niev Pleimouth (Plymouth), Quebec, Virginia, C. May (Cape May), New France (Canada), Noorst Rivier al Maritins Rivier (Hudson River), Fort Orange (now Albany), and New Amsterdam, which became New York City. A number of Indian tribes are listed by name: Pequatoos (Pequots), Morhicans (Mohicans), and Matouwacs (Montauks).

The captions for the Indians in canoes on the Mar del Norte (North Sea or North Atlantic) are in Latin and note that the canoes are made from dug-out trees. Some of the features are not accurate, reflecting the lack of knowledge at the time. The St. Lawrence River west of Quebec is too far to the south; the Lacus Irocoisiensis (now Lake Champlain) is too large, a common mistake at the time; the Appalachian Mountains do not extend beyond a small area in what is now New York and New Hampshire. Some English words (Bay, Point) are used to describe geographical features along with Dutch words that are similar to their English counterparts – zee (sea), and eylandt (island). One of the Dutch names that has survived and is in use today is Tappaens, for a tribe of Indians. The Tappan Zee Bridge spans the Hudson River today in this area north of New York City.

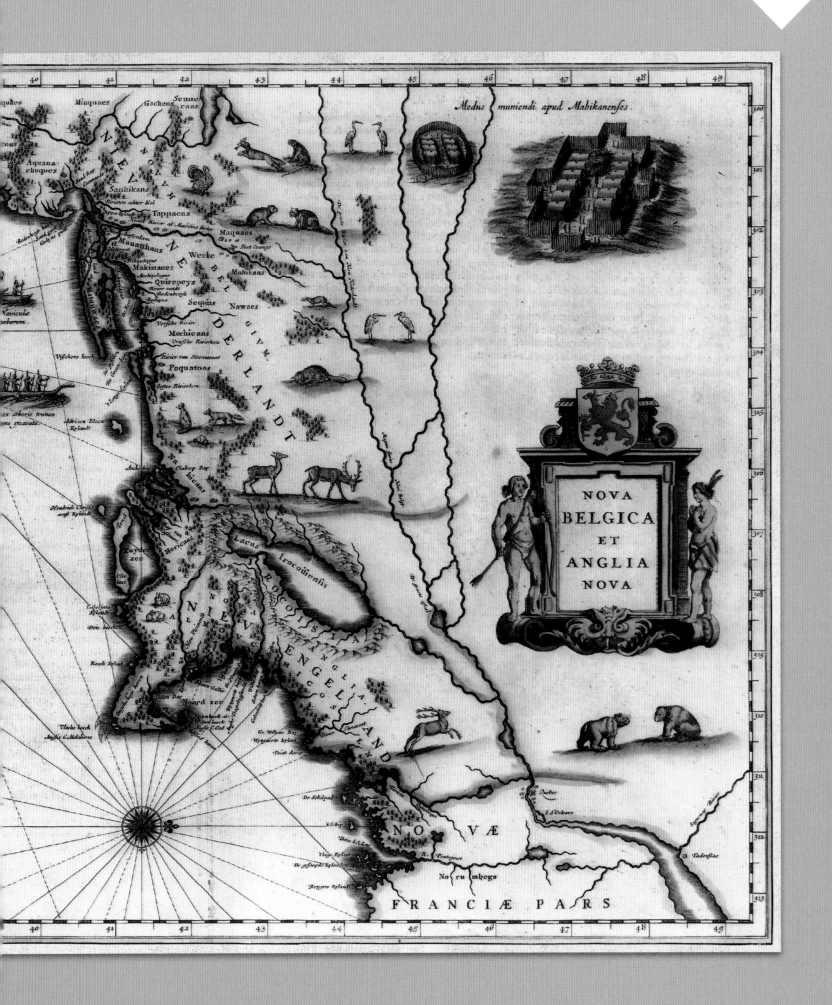

CONQUISTADORS &
THE TRIBES OF THE SOUTHWEST

THE EARLY EUROPEAN EXPLORERS OF WESTERN NORTH AMERICA
ARRIVED FROM ALL DIRECTIONS. BESIDES SEA-GOING EXPLORATIONS
OF THE NORTHWEST COAST THERE WERE INCURSIONS DOWN THE
MISSISSIPPI VALLEY BY THE FRENCH (STARTING WITH LASALLE IN
1682) AND, LATER, BY THE BRITISH IN PURSUIT OF THE FUR TRADE.

But the first whites to penetrate the southwest were the Spanish conquistadors ("conquerors"), who began to explore the northern part of the continent after Spain established a presence in the New World in the early sixteenth century. These were men of influence who presented their cases before Spanish royalty for the glory of God, their king, and themselves.

ABOVE Francisco Vásquez de Coronado and his expedition trudge along the Arkansas River in present-day Oklahoma in his final attempt to find "El Dorado," a place of gold. His journey took him as far as Kansas before he turned back.

Intrigue prevented Hernando de Cortés, the great conquistador of Mexico, from receiving royal approval for his expedition north from Mexico City, the capital of New Spain. Instead, the mission fell to a young and influential soldier-aristocrat, Francisco Vásquez de Coronado, who intended to search for a legendary place of fabulous wealth in gold, the Seven Cities of Cibola, reportedly seen by the off-course survivors of an earlier Spanish expedition from Florida. Coronado followed a trail blazed by a French monk and his guides in 1539 who laid claim to the land for Spain. With a well-equipped group of soldiers and civilians, Coronado set out the following year on a route paralleling the west coast of Mexico, with plans to rendezvous with two ships looking for a northern passage in the Southern Sea (the Pacific Ocean). The original plan was frustrated when the ships sailed to the head of the Sea of Cortés (Gulf of California) and, unable to proceed, turned back.

Though the land route proved difficult, Coronado's expedition made it to the mythical seven cities, which were actually the Indian pueblos at Zuni, only to find the monk's reports were greatly exaggerated. Further exploration revealed the fertile valley of the Rio Grande River in New Mexico, where Coronado and his men were trapped for the winter. Friction with the natives led to the condemnation to death of 200 Indians. The following spring, the Pueblo Indians (whose name derives from the Spanish word for a small town) convinced

THE HORSE

The horse, a food source for Paleo-Indian hunters, disappeared from the continent in the Ice Age, but thousands of years later would become the most important non-game animal of Native American life when reintroduced by the Spanish conquistadors. The southwestern tribes were the first to adapt the horse for draft and transportation, stealing or gathering in stray animals from their European conquerors and copying their use. These tribes then started a vigorous trade with their neighbors to the north and gradually the trade worked its way east of the Rockies, and into the hands of the Great Plains tribes with whom the horse has been most closely identified.

Coronado to continue his search east and his expedition got as far as Kansas but never found the El Dorado ("gold-laden" place) which they sought. In 1542 Coronado retraced his steps back to Mexico, never to return. It would be 56 years before Don Juan de Oñate led an expedition to New Mexico and established the first permanent settlement there.

The Pueblo tribes encountered by Coronado were descendents of one of three main Indian groups of the semi-arid southwest, the Anasazi. They are discussed in more depth on pages 16–17. The other two groups were the Mogollón and the Hohokam. The Mogollón, who were primarily gatherers, lived in caves or brush dwellings in the high country of the southwest and developed

ABOVE A wider view of the Canyon de Chelly ruins. As a result of increased raiding when the Civil War began, in 1863–64 U. S. soldiers under militia colonel Kit Carson rounded up more than 8,000 Navajos from their homes in Canyon de Chelly and marched them to the Bosque Redondo Reservation in eastern New Mexico. They were returned to their homes after the war.

ABOVE The west portion of a once expansive three-story pueblo in northwestern New Mexico called Aztec Ruins. Pueblo Indians built the 500-room structure at the height of the early pueblo phase about A.D. 1100. Although the Spanish explored here, the incorrect reference to these Native Americans as Aztecs was made by nineteenth-century Americans who came to the area.

IRRIGATION

The basis of modern agriculture in the southwest United States is irrigation. This was developed by the Hohokam and adopted by their descendants. The Hohokam tapped the Gila River and its tributaries to bring water to their maize fields. Their engineering technique was deceptively simple; they let the water flow into the canals as they dug, using the depth of water they stood in to judge whether each channel was too shallow or too deep. Later, the Pimas used the irrigation canals to expand their crop line from maize to include squash and kidney beans, and to achieve great yields of wheat.

ABOVE A Navajo hogán, a traditional mud hut supported by wooden poles, overlooks a family cornfield in Holbrook, Arizona. The former raiders adapted successfully to agriculture after learning it from the Pueblo Indians whom they targeted in raids.

the art of basket-making. Later, they embraced agriculture and began to congregate in villages of small numbers, building round or squared houses of logs with a base dug three to four feet into the ground. Their culture flourished from around 200 B.C.–A.D. 1000. Their descendents are members of the Hopi tribe.

The only early culture of North American Indians to embrace crop farming for their entire food needs also lived in the most arid region of the subcontinent. The Hohokam were wanderers from Mexico who settled in the Gila River valley between 2000 and 200 B.C. What made them so successful was their use of that river's water to irrigate their crops. They spoke two languages, Piman and Yuman. The Piman speakers, by the eighteenth century, had become the Pima and Papagos tribes. They subsisted on crops, wild plants, small game and fish, and were generally friendly to the whites who passed through their villages in large numbers on the trail to California. The Yuman speakers developed into the Yuma, Mohave, Havasupai, and other semi-nomadic tribes that settled the Colorado River area of what is now Arizona and California. The most successful planters, such as the Havasupai, established trade with their less agriculturally successful neighbors.

To the east of the Hohokam descendants were a group of more recent Athapaskan-speaking arrivals to the New World, the Apaches. They were nomads, like the tribes of the southern plains with whom they would intermix, the Comanches and the Kiowa. Raiders, they preyed on neighboring tribes and, eventually, on the white man. Another Athapaskan-speaking tribe, the Navajo, settled the mountainous area where New Mexico's boundary now joins three other states. They combined aggressive raiding on their Pueblo neighbors with successful agriculture. Their location in this isolated section of the southwest, and their environment, would eventually lead them to become the largest tribe in North America.

TOP LEFT Casa Grande (Great House), a four-story edifice near Phoenix that was at the center of Hohokam culture. The unique development of irrigation ditches fed by the Gila and Salt Rivers allowed these late Archaic People to cultivate plants in a harsh arid environment.

ABOVE LEFT Gila Cliff Dwellings National Monument preserves dwellings of the Mogollón culture including rock shelters, pit houses and this pueblo edifice built in a cliff under an expansive mesa. During their existence the Mogollón lived in the area from this location in southwestern New Mexico through west Texas and northern Mexico.

ABOVE A detailed portion of Casa Grande. The structure is the largest known example of their caliche (sand, clay, and limestone mixture) architecture and was reinforced with timbers floated down the nearby Gila River. The ceremonial building is oriented to the four cardinal compass points and openings in the walls allowed the sun and moon to enter at cyclical times, giving seasonal information useful to these agriculturalists.

THE EFFECTS OF ENGLISH & FRENCH COLONIZATION

THE IDYLLIC IMAGE OF A THANKSGIVING FEAST, IN
WHICH NATIVE AMERICANS AND WHITE SETTLERS
CELEBRATED A SUCCESSFUL HARVEST SEASON, BELIES
THE OFTEN BLOODY AND MOSTLY DEADLY EFFECTS
OF FRENCH AND ENGLISH COLONIZATION
ON THE NATIVES OF NORTH AMERICA.

ABOVE Sa Ga Yeath Qua Pieth Tow, king of the Maquas (Mohawks), was one of the four Iroquois chiefs to go to London in 1710. The Jan Verelst paintings of the kings hung in Kensington Palace and John Simon produced mezzotint engravings from them for distribution.

The feast probably did take place, a result of the sheltering of the Plymouth Colony by Chief Massasoit of the Wampanoag tribe in 1621 who was seeking allies against his enemy the Narraganset. From the early exploration by England's John Cabot at the end of the fifteenth century, North America became a prize to be competed over by England, France and, to a lesser extent, other European countries. Even before colonization began, European explorers and fishermen who dropped anchor along the Atlantic Coast and entered its inlets became a source of curiosity and disease for the American natives. The problem of disease was aggravated as France and England, seeing the riches of gold, silver, and other valuables brought from the New World by the Spanish galleons they captured, created chartered companies to colonize North America.

England first claimed a colony in Newfoundland in 1583 to aid its fishing interests there. The Virginia Company, led by Sir Walter Raleigh, was granted a charter by Queen Elizabeth I with the provision of being able to take any land inhabited by non-Christians. The colony which was established on Roanoke Island, now part of North Carolina, in 1585 lasted

POCAHONTAS

Pocahontas was born Matowaka, but her father, the powerful chief Powhatan, referred to her as Pakahantes meaning "my favorite daughter." Captain John Smith claimed that the teenage girl put herself between him and the executioner's axe when Smith was a Powhatan captive. Whether or not this is true, she became the most famous Native American female among Europeans in the seventeenth century. In 1612 she was held hostage by the English and fell in love with and married the colonist John Rolfe. Powhatan kept peace with the colonists until his death in 1618. Pocahontas became a Christian, sailed to England and was presented to the Court of King Charles I but died of smallpox in 1617 before returning to the colonies. Her son, Thomas Rolfe, was one of the most powerful leaders of colonial Virginia.

> "Where the English come to settle, a Divine Hand makes way for them, by removing or cutting off the Indians, either by Wars one with the other, or by some raging mortal Disease."
>
> Daniel Denton, 1670

ABOVE Pocahontas interceding for the life of Captain John Smith in 1608. Although the English ungratefully kidnapped her four years later to ransom peace with her father Powhatan, Pocahontas became the first widely known Native American celebrity in Europe.

only three years, its survivors captured or melded into the local native population.

The next attempt by the Virginia Company would be at Jamestown in 1607. The difficult conditions nearly led the colony to founder. Among their troubles were attacks by warriors from the Pamunkey and other members of the 200-village Powhatan Confederacy. The colony survived in part when the confederation's leader, Powhatan, made peace with the Virginia Company after his daughter, Pocahontas, married an Englishman in 1612. Trade began and tobacco was discovered, a cash crop that would ultimately lead to a prosperous Virginia. After Powhatan's death in 1618, a wave of violence spread, breaking out in 1622 and again 22 years later. By that time, however, the colonists greatly outnumbered the Indians and the Native American fate in the region was effectively sealed.

In the seventeenth century the French began to found colonies in what is now Nova Scotia and at the mouth of the St. Lawrence River. New France took on permanence when Samuel de Champlain established Québec in 1608. At that time the powerful Huron tribe controlled the area. The French brought Catholic missionaries with them, but it would be many years before they obtained any converts to the Catholic religion. As French influence spread over eastern Canada, fur trading quickly became a viable industry. The Iroquois Confederacy was being wooed by the Dutch who were establishing their own colonial settlements in the Hudson River valley. Competition between the English of the rapidly

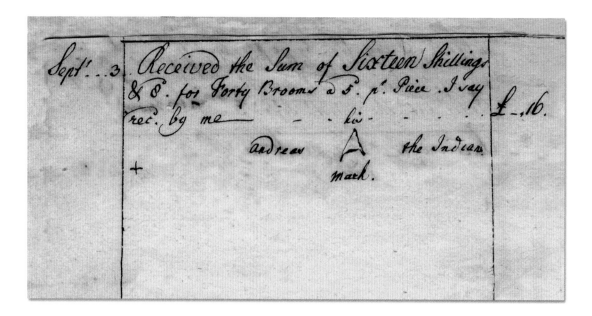

ABOVE This goods receipt indicates that on September 3, 1759, a Native American named Andreas received the sum of 16 shillings and 8 pence for 40 brooms at 5 pence each.

expanding colonies of New England and the Dutch caused the Iroquois to wage war on neighboring tribes as the demands of the fur trade outran the supply the Confederacy could muster on their own lands.

They attacked the tribes to the south, including the Delaware, and to the north, challenging the Huron along the St. Lawrence and conquering the Erie in 1654. Meanwhile, French traders established posts in the Great Lakes region to extend their trade and power. Raids and devastating wars broke out in other areas of the colonies as the European powers used intertribal warfare to consolidate their own gains in power and land, as occurred during the War of the Spanish Succession (1701–14).

OPPOSITE Samuel de Champlain, seen here offering gifts to Indians in Canada, took three ships up the St. Lawrence River and established a trading post, Quebec, in 1608. By 1615 he had explored west to the Great Lakes and, allied with the Huron tribe, battled Iroquois in Ontario. He was wounded in this action in which the Huron were defeated and Iroquois power again surged over Canada.

ABOVE William Penn's treaty with the Indians under the elm tree at Shackamaxon, in what is now Pennsylvania, represented the Quaker leader's honest attempt to make peace with the tribes in his proprietorship. However, his son would undermine his father's fair dealings with Indians when he came to power.

BOW AND ARROW

In the early days of the Jamestown Settlement, an Englishman challenged a friendly native to shoot an arrow through a leather-covered wood shield about three feet in diameter.

To the astonishment of the European, the arrow dug a foot deep into the target. Sometime in the Archaic period, Native Americans discovered that animal sinew could be stretched and dried, attached to a flexible piece of wood and used to propel a stone-tipped stick through the air. European metal made arrow tips more deadly. Even after the introduction of firearms, many warriors preferred the time-tested bow and arrow for horseback hunting and warfare.

ABOVE Four examples of chipped stone arrowheads. Arrowheads were produced by nearly every North American Indian tribe from the Archaic Stage forward, including the Algonquian and Iroquoian speakers of the eastern and central Woodlands.

HUDSON RIVER DEED

This deed for land along New York's Hudson River was signed with the marks of five Native American chiefs. Each is accompanied by a wax seal.

DELAWARE RIVER DEED (OPPOSITE)

This deed dated 5 May, 1681, is between Towies Alom and Patascus, of an unspecified Indian tribe, probably the Nanicoke, and covers a tract of land in the Delaware River valley. The 1681 deed, in English, indicates a tract of land sold by nine Indians who are named in the "bargain," what today would be called a contract, and Hans Seiessen Palascus and Ceran Ipeece, two white men. The tract is described by the creeks which form its borders. A map on the verso indicates these borders, an Indian village and possibly the land of a white neighbour. There is mention of one geographical feature, schilpakill, which could be the Schuylkill River. The Schuylkill flows through what is now eastern Pennsylvania and Philadelphia and into the Delaware River. The only discernable mention of compensation for the land is "two halfe anchors of Licquor." Mention is made of the "hunting, fishing and fowling" on the land as part of the deal. The document indicates its validity "for ourselves and all heirs and assigns," language still used in modern legal contracts. The document was apparently prepared by someone who was able to communicate its tenets to the Indians, who used their marks to indicate their agreement with the pact.

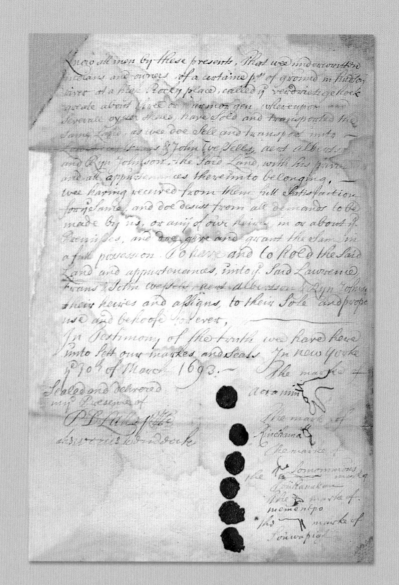

Wee undernamed Alom: Lolichetin, Towies
Lalebachkinna, or sickhethay Pickao, Sichalandy, o' sideres
& for Conockele Palickthen & petkastink being
all of us y naturall owners & proprietors of y Land Indian
Lying in y Grandewyns faalls in Cristina Creeke
Dod hereby Declare to haue bargained Sould & —
made ouer & dod by these pdsents for o' Selues &
o' heyrs & assignes Bargaine Sell & make ouer
unto Hans Peiersen Palascus: a certain peece
of Land Lying & being bitweene, y Creeke called
Silakonck & y Creeke called Kithantennissink —
beginning att a small branch w'h runs out of Silakonck
Creeke & so up along y said Silakonck or Grandewyn —
Creeke as farr as another small rim called alapockos
rim & from thence ouer to another Rim w'h —
belong to Kithantennissink or y schilpa kill & so
downe y Rim as far as opposit to y first place
of beginning togei   all y trees & under
        rees Shrubs Grasse & all other priviledges
& benfitts of hunting fishing & fowling there unto
belonging or in any wayes appurtaining. To
haue & to hold y said Land & premisses w'h all & singular
y appurtenances unto y sd hans Peidrss his heirs &
assigns for euer;   and wee do hereby declare —
& aknowledge to haue theceived full Sattisfaction
& Content of y sd hans peidrss by twoo halfe anckers
of Liequor & twoo matscoats, to us in hand delivd
with the day hereds above & the this 5 day of
may 1681
            a small map is on y others syd hereof by
            y Indians directions made & the trees are
            by them marked upon y Land;

the marke
of Towies

this is y marke
maad by Lilichetin

This is y
marke of alom
an Indian suching
maad by him
selfe

Turne ouer —

FIRST CONTACT ON THE NORTHWEST COAST

A LONG, NARROW RIBBON OF LAND STRETCHES FROM
THE PENINSULAR REGION OF ALASKA TO JUST BEYOND THE
SOUTHERN BORDER OF TODAY'S OREGON. FACED ON THE EAST
BY THE CASCADE RANGE AND THE NORTHERN REACHES OF THE
ROCKY MOUNTAINS, AND ON THE WEST BY THE PACIFIC OCEAN,
IT IS A REGION OF NATURAL BEAUTY AND RICH RESOURCES.

Into this region came the first people of the future Native American tribes of the northwest. They were probably some of the last to cross the land bridge, and the record of their history goes back 4,000 years. They are people concerned in the utmost with their past, and their ancestral heritage dominates major aspects of their lives.

Hemmed in by the mountains and living on an even narrower strip of rocky coast with only occasional narrow beaches were the Tlingit, Haida, Tsimshian, Kwakiutl, Nootka, Makah, Salish, Quinault, Chinook, and other tribes. They came from three major linguistic stocks: Athapaskan, like their neighbors to the north and east, and two of the more obscure forms of Algonquian. Culturally they shared many traits, however, with lineage and class society being among the most prominent. Another shared trait, almost unheard of in other Native American cultures, was a complete lack of agriculture.

ABOVE Fort Vancouver, on the Columbia River, near its confluence with the Willamette River, in present-day Washington, began as a trading post and regional headquarters for the Hudson's Bay Company. Pictured in this woodcut is its later incarnation as a U.S. Army outpost.

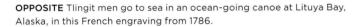

OPPOSITE Tlingit men go to sea in an ocean-going canoe at Lituya Bay, Alaska, in this French engraving from 1786.

ABOVE A shell necklace of Nuu-chah-nulth origin from 1780.

With 100 inches (250 cm) of annual rainfall and a mild and moist climate determined by the mountain barrier and warm Japanese Current offshore, there was no need for it. Fauna was abundant in the dense evergreen forests, and aquatic food sources were even more readily available.

Besides hunting, fishing, and the occasional gathering of wild plants for food, another environmental factor defined the culture. The forests of pine, spruce, and especially red and yellow cedar made these tribes woodcrafters of superlative ability. Their skill was not only utilitarian, for the construction of dwellings and water-craft, but also possessed an aesthetic sense for sophisticated carving and crafting techniques. With simple non-metallic tools, these woodworkers cut and carved houses up to 60 feet (18 m) in length, canoes which ranged in size up to the same upper limit, fashioned from a single downed tree, and hundreds of other useful and decorative items. They traveled by canoe on the rivers and open sea in search of food and as war parties, which were usually assembled for acquiring slaves, or occasionally for retribution of some wrong caused by an affront to a village chief.

TOTEM POLES

The totem pole as a free-standing carved wooden representation of northwest Indian culture is a fairly recent phenomenon, appearing around the early nineteenth century. Originally the carved cedar logs were produced as center posts and entrances to the large wooden houses in which kinfolk and clans coexisted. The animal figures represented the family crest of the house and occasionally tributes to the deeds of departed relatives. Whites became fascinated with them and the poles were adapted as free-standing signposts to villages and the clans and kinfolk that inhabited and, therefore, controlled stretches of the coastline. Although originally denounced by church and government as pagan symbols, the twentieth century saw a rebirth of the totem pole as a cultural symbol.

First contact came with the explorers who arrived in the small inlets around the upper peninsula of Washington and Vancouver Island in 1775. A lively trade developed and, while there was some individual strife over cheating on both sides, the bartering flourished and soon the metal objects, cloth, and bright colored bangles brought by the European ships were redistributed to tribes in exchange for pelts, woodcarvings, and pearls. One tribe on the southern edge of the culture, the Chinooks, already had a reputation as a trading band, and the new goods they acquired enhanced this, since they traded not only along the northwest coast, but also with the tribes of northern California and the plateau region. The tribes of the northwest coast never engaged in full-scale war with the whites, although several groups of skirmishes occuring in the nineteenth century, such as Kamiakin's War, reached larger proportions as missionaries, settlers, and government intrusion began to affect their long-established ways of life.

ABOVE This wooden double chest is of Tsimshian origin, a tribe from northern British Columbia. It is carved on four sides to represent a mythical sea monster.

ABOVE A camp of Chinook Indians at The Dalles, Oregon on the Columbia River. Fish dry on one of the tent poles. Mount Hood is pictured in the background.

ABOVE A Quinault girl wears ornaments made of shells meticulously strung together in this Edward Curtis photograph.

THE POTLATCH

One of the most fascinating and contradictory aspects of the northwest coast Native American culture was the Potlatch, from the Nootka word "give." The Potlatch was a great feast in which a family chief and his clan expended a stockpile of goods that had been accumulated for months (sometimes years) to stage a large feast, often as part of a wedding or coming-of-age ceremony, for invited guests from another clan or village. The result of the potlatch sometimes sunk a chief into a period of indigence. For a culture in which chiefs measured status by the accumulation of wealth, this seems incongruous behavior. Yet there was a catch. The guest chief and his clan would be expected to repay their host, with interest, in the form of an even larger feast with more gifts at some time in the future.

ABOVE This interior of a Coast Salish dwelling was painted by Paul Kane, one of the talented nineteenth-century painters who portrayed Native American life. He spent time among the Coast Salish in 1847. Here, one woman spins while another weaves a blanket. The raw materials for these textiles were wool from the mountain goat and hair from a specially bred dog (pictured). That breed is now extinct.

SPANISH COLONIZATION OF NEW MEXICO

OF ALL THE TRIBES OF THE ARID SOUTHWEST, THE ANASAZI (NAVAJO FOR "OLD ONES") WERE THE MOST ARCHITECTURALLY PROLIFIC. BUT THE FAMILIAR ADOBE PUEBLO WAS NOT THE INITIAL DWELLING OF THESE PEOPLE OF THE DESERT TRADITION THAT WERE INFLUENCED BY HOHOKAM AND MOLLOGÓN TRADITIONS BUT WERE DISTINCT IN OTHER WAYS.

Geographically they inhabited the Four Corners area where present-day Colorado, New Mexico, Utah, and Arizona join. Chronologically, the culture began about A.D. 1 and at the time the dwellings were rounded mud huts, partially subterranean. Their culture prospered on good maize growing with ample summer rains. Gradually they underwent a change that caused them to abandon their semi-subterranean houses for square houses of dried adobe or adobe bricks. By A.D. 750 these homes were joined by common walls and even stacked as kin and clans lived in adjoining units in the desert canyons.

By A.D. 1050 the pueblos had evolved into large villages. Pueblo Bonita in Chaco Canyon, for example, had 800 units. But the competition among pueblos led to the abandonment of the canyon homes and the Anasazi migrated to the cliffs of the mesas, building the same compartmentalized dwelling villages on top of high plateaus, or in protected areas of the mesa cliffs.

TOP AND RIGHT Hopi dwellings at Walpi. On a group of mesas in northeastern Arizona sit the eight pueblo communities who speak Hopi and one pueblo of refugees from Spanish occupation of the Rio Grande valley.

ABOVE A Navajo hogán in Window Rock, Arizona. The hogán was traditionally earthen and built over three large poles covered by brush with two smaller poles making an eastward-facing doorway. The floor was dug about a foot (30 cm) deep to provide an interior bench along the walls. This improvement on the old style features some horizontal log substructure, but is still earth-covered.

OPPOSITE Navajo men on horseback in the mesa-studded Four Corners area. The Navajo were among the first to acquire horses through raiding the pueblos to which horses were introduced by the Spanish. The Navajo funneled horse trade to the tribes of the Rockies.

The climate was changing and about three hundred years later these dwellings were also abandoned. Most clans settled in the fertile Rio Grande valley of northern New Mexico and areas of west Texas. The Anasazi as a culture gave way to the pueblo tribes in these areas, including the Hopi, who established villages in northeast Arizona, and the Zuni, who established a large community midway between the Hopi and the Rio Grande valley settlers.

It was the Zuni pueblo that was the subject of stories told by survivors of a disastrous Spanish mission to Florida who traveled overland to the west and finally to Mexico. Called the Seven Cities of Cibola, it was the first southwestern community visited by Francisco Vásquez de Coronado in 1540. Finding the reports of those who preceded him greatly exaggerated, Coronado moved

PUEBLO DRESS

The modern Pueblo Native American wears a combination of traditional and western-style clothing. The men wear a cotton shirt over a pair of cotton trousers that end just below the knees. A sash, usually yellow, or leather belt with silver adornment is worn round the waist. The more traditional breech cloth or G-string is only used for ceremonial purposes, along with a feather headdress. The women wear a rectangular woolen garment in black or brown called a manta which is tied over the right shoulder and under the left arm. It is often decorated at the hem with red or blue trim. A hemmed skirt is worn underneath, tied with a sash at the waist, and from the Spanish influence a slip is worn underneath and an apron in front, and perhaps a shawl. Both sexes use blanket wraps for cold weather and wear hard moccasins, the women preferring white moccasins or boots. Hopi maidens often wear their hair in the symbolic butterfly style shown here.

ABOVE A Navajo first-phase chief-style blanket (early 1800s) of handspun churro wool. An archeological discovery dates this technique in patterns of horizontal stripes of white, brown, and indigo to 1750 or earlier. Navajo blankets were in great demand as social expressions, and in trade. Plains Indians would trade as many as ten bison robes for a quality blanket.

east and spent the winter among the pueblos in the Rio Grande valley. The Pueblo Indians sent Coronado east in his search for gold and were rid of the Spanish for 60 years.

Then an expedition of Spanish and Mexican Indians arrived under the command of Juan de Oñate to colonize the Rio Grande Valley. At first the pueblo dwellers were satisfied with a peaceful coexistence side by side with the newcomers and even allowed the building of Catholic churches among the pueblos. The traditional place for the Indians to meditate, socialize and conduct spiritual ceremonies was the kiva, a rounded and domed adobe room reminiscent of the original Anasazi dwellings. An open hole in the roof represented the ascendancy of man into the Upper World. But the Spanish friars insisted the Indians abandon their traditional beliefs and submit to their strict form of Christianity with harsh punishment for those who didn't.

At dawn on August 10, 1680 the Pueblo Indians and some of the mixed-blood immigrants revolted against the oppression of the missionaries, slaughtering about 400 Spaniards. The survivors fled to Sante Fe, then El Paso. Another expedition arrived 12 years later and offered coexistence of the two cultures. The pueblo people compromised as well, accepting some principles of Christianity while practicing their traditional religion. For the remaining few years of the sixteenth century and the next two centuries, the Pueblo Indians were mostly unaffected by the changing political landscape of the region, and they remain the most settled in their ancestral lands and culture of all North American Indians.

LEFT A Kachina doll in the form of a group of *koshares* (sacred clowns), participating in a pueblo ceremony. The *koshares* were painted from head to foot in black and white stripes with their hair tied with corn husks. They channeled the spirit of fertility in dances and provided comic relief during ceremonies.

CHEROKEE & OTHER TRIBES & SETTLEMENT OF THE SOUTHEAST

THE APPALACHIAN FOOTHILLS OF THE SOUTHEAST WERE HOME TO THE DYNAMIC TRIBE OF IROQUOIAN SPEAKERS KNOWN SINCE FIRST CONTACT AS THE CHEROKEES. THEIR LANDS COMPRISED WHAT ARE NOW PARTS OF WESTERN VIRGINIA, EASTERN KENTUCKY AND TENNESSEE, AND NORTHERN GEORGIA AND ALABAMA.

ABOVE At the end of the Civil War, emancipated slaves formerly owned by Cherokees, such as this mother and child sitting in front of their cabin in Fort Gibson, Indian Territory, became eligible for citizenship in the Cherokee Nation.

Like their distant Iroquois relatives to the north, they were a maternally-based culture, with clans forming around the women, who also selected leadership positions in the mostly democratic tribal council. The females owned the lands and thatched-roof dwellings that were scattered among many small clan-based villages. They were successful farmers, fishermen in the fresh water streams running down from the mountains, and hunters of all kinds of game. The Cherokees' neighbors to the east were the Algonquian-speaking Catawba, while to the west and south were the Muskogean speakers, the Choctaws, Chickasaws, and Creeks. The latter was a name given by the colonists because the Creek villages were usually found on river banks. They had a semi-socialistic culture in which a supreme ruler, a mico, was appointed for life, but had no absolute power. He was advised by a group of senior tribesmen in community affairs. Like the Cherokees, the Creeks had a maternal predominance. Intermarriage was strictly taboo, and clans were identified with animal names. The socialistic aspect of their culture was the practice of communal, as well as individual, agriculture for visitors and the indigent. Some Creek villages were peaceful and others warlike. The Choctaw and Chickasaw cultures were in many respects similar to that of

HARVEST FESTIVAL

Because of favorable climatic conditions, the agricultural output of southeastern tribes was usually abundant. The great importance they placed on the gods for their agricultural success is manifested in their celebration of harvest festivals. At the four-day green corn festival or "busk" celebrated by the Creeks, all old clothing and household goods were burned and replaced by new items. All criminal offenders except for murderers were pardoned and the community feasted on deer and the new crop of maize. Games were played, including the original form of lacrosse, and dances were held. Men underwent ritual cleansing by imbibing an herbal drink.

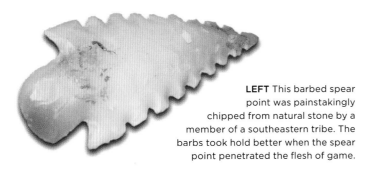

LEFT This barbed spear point was painstakingly chipped from natural stone by a member of a southeastern tribe. The barbs took hold better when the spear point penetrated the flesh of game.

the Creek. These two tribes resided principally in what are now Mississippi and southern Alabama.

When trouble began with the neighboring Catawba and Creek tribes, the Cherokees formed larger villages and pacts between them to fight their enemies. Contact with Europeans heightened the friction between the groups. As French and British trappers and traders entered the region in the eighteenth century, the Cherokee aligned themselves with one or the other. The Creeks favored the British, but a group split off from the tribe and eventually became the Seminoles. European trade goods empowered tribal leaders, and a great deal of intermarriage began between the English and Scottish men who came into the region and Creek and Cherokee women. The offspring of these unions were readily accepted into the tribe. Well armed with British muskets by the time of the American Revolution, the Cherokee, incensed by the influx of settlers, fought for the British against the colonists and their allies, the

ABOVE Elias Boudinot (Buck Watie) was a highly educated member of an influential Cherokee family. He assumed his new name from a member of the Continental Congress who took an interest in him. Boudinot was the first editor of the *Cherokee Phoenix* and worked tirelessly for the education of his people. One of the Cherokees who were resigned early on to the forced move to Indian Territory, he was executed there on June 22, 1839, by a faction of Cherokees who viewed his acceptance of the government movement order as treason.

Catawba. The Creeks, Choctaw, and Chickasaws tried to stay out of the wars between white men.

By the end of the War of Independence, the strongest community of Cherokees was situated in northwest Georgia, centering around a settlement on the Etowah River. Even though they maintained their tribal independence, the Cherokee assimilated European culture, language, clothing, and education to a great degree. Some expanded their agricultural holdings into plantation size, grew and traded cash crops, and even owned slaves. Eventually they signed treaties with the new American government and fought alongside Andrew Jackson in the hope of maintaining their ancestral lands. But that hope would be dashed despite their ambitious political and diplomatic efforts to influence their own destiny.

ABOVE RIGHT Joseph Vann was a wealthy mixed-blood Cherokee who was well capitalized when he made the move to Indian Territory. At one point he had 110 slaves working on his plantation and steamboat business. A notorious drinker and gambler, Vann lost his life and those of 52 other souls on his paddle-wheeler Lucy Walker when the vessel's boiler blew up during a high-stakes race with another steamer on the Ohio River in 1844.

RIGHT This 1885 illustration by John White of Pomeioc village in North Carolina shows a typical southeastern village, with bark lodges built in a circular pattern around a common area.

BELOW RIGHT The Cherokee nation was split on slavery. Many Cherokees brought their slaves with them to Indian Territory, traded slaves, and offered rewards for the capture of runaways, as this 1845 announcement in the *Cherokee Advocate* attests. But other Cherokees harbored the fugitives until the Confederate defeat in the Civil War sealed their emancipation.

SEQUOYAH

Sequoyah, also known as George Geist, was a Cherokee of mixed blood, with a German trader father and Native American mother. He was raised in the Cherokee culture and supposedly never learned English. After a crippling accident, he devised an alphabet of the Cherokee language that was made up of about 80 characters. It was enthusiastically accepted and widely studied. Many Cherokees became literate, and in 1828 the first Native American weekly newspaper was printed. The inaugural issue included Sequoyah's thoughts promoting the Cherokee ideal of independent sovereignty.

$20 REWARD.

RANAWAY on the 21st September last, from the subscriber, living on Grand river, near the mouth of Honey creek, Cherokee Nation, a negro man named ALLEN, who is about 25 years old, about 5 feet 2 or 3 inches high; very black; has very white eyes; rather a stoppage in his speech when speaking, and a wen under his thigh. When he left he had on a plaid shirt and copperas colored pantaloons; and also, marks of the whip, inflicted before he came into my possession.

Any person arresting and returning the said negro to me or lodging him in jail so that I can get him, will receive a reward of twenty dollars.

PETER HILDEBRAND.
Cherokee Nation, Oct. 22—2w.

Cherokee Temperance Societies.

☞ The Secretaries of the several Temperance Societies in the Nation, are respectfully requested, to forward, immediately, to the undersigned, a list of the names of all persons who have united with their respective Societies during the past year; and also any other information that may be valuable, or interesting, connected with the progress of Temperance among the Cherokees, within the same time.   WILL. P. ROSS,
        Sec. Cher. Tem. Society.
Sept. 25, 1845.

NOTICE.

THERE will be sold to the highest bidder, on Saturday, the fifteenth of December next, at Webber's Salt Works, the following named NEGROES, to wit: CHARLOTTE, MARY AND her two CHILDREN; RACHAEL AND HER CHILD, and one Negro Man. All of which will be sold for the purpose of making an equal division of the proceeds of said negroes among the heirs of Ruth Phillip, deceased.

☞ Terms of sale Cash. Sale to commence at 12 o'clock.

LOONEY PRICE.
ELLIS PHILLIPS.
Sept. 18, 1845—2-tds.

LEFT The *Cherokee Phoenix* newspaper began publication in 1828 with parallel columns in English and the Cherokee language devised by Sequoyah. It was a significant attribute of the Cherokee culture when it was at its apex in Georgia, and dealt with issues important to the Cherokees, including their freedom. Most of the newspaper is bilingual, that is, the information is given in English and Cherokee. A few details of the news and editorial pieces are different in the two languages, but they essentially cover the same information. The verses are biblical passages and a Cherokee hymn, important to Christianized Cherokees. The *Cherokee Phoenix* is still in publication.

ABOVE This pipe carved in the shape of a duck was found in Georgia's Clay County, an area where there are also burial mounds. It is made from steatite, a popular stone used in early carvings.

CHEROKEE TREATY 1835

The Cherokee treaty of 1835 was known as the Treaty of New Echota, after the Georgia capital of the Cherokee Nation. It was arranged by the administration of Andrew Jackson, who was a leading figure in driving the Cherokee from their lands east of the Mississippi River. Among the signatories was long-time chief Major Ridge who had been instrumental in helping Jackson defeat the Red Sticks at the Battle of Horseshoe Bend. Given that a large number of Cherokees vehemently opposed the treaty, Ridge commented as he affixed his mark to the document, "I have signed my death warrant."

purpose as soon after the ratification of this Treaty as an appropriation for the same shall be made. It is however not intended in this Article to interfere with that part of the Annuities due the Cherokees west by the Treaty of 1819

Article 19 This treaty after the same shall be ratified by the President & Senate of the United States shall be obligatory on the contracting parties.

In testimony whereof the Commissioners and the Chiefs head men & people whose names are hereunto annexed being duly authorized by the people in general council assembled have affixed their hands & seals for themselves & in behalf of the Cherokee Nation. I have examined the foregoing treaty and altho' not present when it was made, approving its provisions generally, and therefore sign it.

Cue te hee   his mark   [Seal]   Wm Carroll [Seal]

Te gah e ske   his mark   [Seal]   J. F. Schermerhorn [Seal]

Robert Rogers   [Seal]   Major Ridge   his mark   [Seal]
John Gunter   [Seal]   James Foster   his mark   [Seal]
John A. Bell   [Seal]   Tesa taesky   his mark   [Seal]
Charles F. Foreman   [Seal]   Charles Moore his mark   [Seal]
William Rogers   [Seal]   George Chambers his mark   [Seal]
George W. Adair   [Seal]   Tah yeske   his mark   [Seal]
Elias Boudinot   [Seal]   Archilla Smith his mark   [Seal]
James Starr   his mark   [Seal]   Andrew Ross   [Seal]
Jesse Halfbreed his mark   [Seal]   William Lasley   [Seal]

Signed & Sealed in
Presence of
Western B Thomas Secy
Ben F. Currey Special Agent
M Wolf Baten as
Lut 6 U.S. Iny Disby Agent
Jno H. Mosier
Aumit & Sufft
C M Hitchcock M.D.
Asst Surgn U.S Army
Jn Currey
Wm H Underwood
Cornelius D Terhune
John W.A Underwood

In compliance with Instructions of the Council
at New Echota we sign this Treaty—
March 1st 1836
Witnesses
Elbert Herring
Alexander H. Everett
John Robb
D Kurtz
Wm Y Hansell
Saml J Potts
Jno Little
S Rockwell

Stand Watie
John Ridge

SEMINOLES & THE DISCOVERY OF FLORIDA

EVEN THOUGH THEY ARE POPULARLY SEEN AS THE TRIBE MOST ASSOCIATED WITH FLORIDA, THE SEMINOLES (SIM-A-NO'LE, MEANING "RUNAWAYS") WERE ACTUALLY AN OFFSHOOT OF THE MUSKOGEAN-SPEAKING CREEKS WHO "DISCOVERED" FLORIDA IN THE EARLY EIGHTEENTH CENTURY.

Long before them, other tribes—the Guale, Apalachee, Timucua, Tekesta, and Calusa—inhabited the Florida panhandle and peninsula. Other than water-borne trading

ABOVE LEFT Nea-Math-La was a Seminole chief during the Second Seminole War. In 1836 he was captured by Alabama militiamen and sent in chains to Indian Territory.

ABOVE RIGHT Billy Bowlegs, the Seminole warrior known as the "Alligator Chief." Bowlegs fought in the Second Seminole War and was among a group that took refuge in the Everglades. They were left alone for a few years until trouble began as white settlement greatly increased in south Florida. He led Seminoles resisting removal against the U.S. government in 1857 but was captured and removed to Indian Territory in 1858. Bowlegs was a skilled diplomat and spoke three languages—and was not, in fact, bowlegged.

with tribes from nearby Caribbean islands, these Native Americans had very little contact with the outside world. That changed after Christopher Columbus's discovery in 1492 of Hispaniola in the Caribbean while searching for a western passage to the Far East; his belief that he had reached the East Indies led to the coining of the misnomer "Indians" for Native Americans. Columbus's discoveries resulted in Spanish exploration of the land to the north. Florida was twice explored by Ponce de León (in 1513 and 1521) and invaded by Spanish landing parties on both coasts. Yet the Native American tribes of Florida avoided the fate of their fellow natives in Central and South America until the 1560s, when France sent several ships to northern Florida and Fort Caroline was established on what is now St. John's River.

The Spanish returned in 1565 to found St. Augustine as the first permanent and lasting settlement in Florida. They wiped out their French rivals by destroying Fort Caroline and its relief expedition. The Spanish then sent explorers and Christian missionaries to establish peace and trade with the natives from present-day South Carolina to Pensacola. The inland Creeks, surrounded by enemies, sought Spanish arms and invited Spanish missionaries to their villages in 1681. Within a few years, they had found a better ally in English-speaking traders from South Carolina. These well-armed Creeks then attacked Spanish missions in northern Florida as well as their

DISEASES

Deadly as the muskets and cannon of the Europeans were to Native Americans during the first several centuries of contact, new diseases were more fatal to the populations of many tribes. Serious diseases such as smallpox, yellow fever, and bubonic plague were unknown in the western hemisphere prior to first contact. Less serious diseases in Europe such as measles, mumps, and whooping cough were often fatal to the Native Americans, who had no immunity to them. A mysterious epidemic spread through New England in 1616–18, killing more than 150,000 Native Americans, including 90 percent of the Wampanoag tribe. The number of Native Americans who died from diseases can only be estimated but it was a major reason for the decline of the population to an all-time low by 1850.

Pre-Contact Diseases
Tuberculosis, Venereal Syphilis

Diseases from Europe
Smallpox, Measles, Cholera, Bubonic Plague, Scarlet Fever, Typhoid, Pleurisy, Diphtheria, Mumps, Whooping Cough, Gonorrhea, Chancroid, Typhus

Diseases from Africa
Malaria, Yellow Fever, Dysentery

Introduced Social Disease
Alcoholism

ABOVE A lithograph of Hernando de Soto and his landing party at Tampa Bay 1539. De Soto not only brought soldiers, but also priests, artisans, tools, and livestock to begin his gold-seeking expedition from an established city, which he called Espiritu Santo, present-day Bradenton. From there he launched a three-year campaign in search of El Dorado, terrorizing, killing, and enslaving Indians along the way, finding no gold, only death, on the banks of the Mississippi River.

Indian enemies to the west. Just after the turn of the eighteenth century, England entered one of the series of wars between European powers, the War of Spanish Succession. In 1702, the English royal governor of South Carolina, James Moore, attempted unsuccessfully to take St. Augustine from the Spanish by force. But his expedition was turned back after a fleet of Spanish ships overtook them. Moore then dispatched Creek war parties to raid St. Augustine and Spanish strongholds. The Creek war parties raided villages of the Florida tribes too and the violence went on in Florida for years. Disease also affected the native Florida tribes and the Seminole invaders. It would be decades before the Seminoles established a strong presence in the area.

By the early 1800s, the Seminoles found themselves facing a new enemy. Andrew Jackson, the hero of the stunning

victory against the British at New Orleans in 1815, had been achieving significant military success against the Indians. After defeating the Red Sticks (northern Creeks) at the Battle of Horseshoe Bend in March 1814 with the aid of southern Creeks and Cherokees, he signed a treaty that gained 20 million acres of Native American land for the United States. In December 1817, President James Madison ordered Jackson to wage war against Creeks and Seminoles in Georgia, under the pretext of preventing runaway slaves from escaping to Florida to join the Seminoles. The campaign was a tacit attempt to gain Florida from the Spanish. Jackson and his Tennessee volunteers were attacked by Seminole warriors near Pensacola, but Jackson eluded the warriors and sacked and destroyed their villages. He then attacked Pensacola, deposed the Spanish governor, and found evidence that Spanish and British subjects there were supplying weapons to the Indians. The First Seminole War ended in 1818 and Spain ceded Florida to the United States in 1819, with Jackson becoming its territorial governor. The Seminoles would continue to fight for decades to maintain their homes in Florida, but most were finally removed, except for a small group that disappeared into the Florida everglades.

ABOVE A colorfully dressed Seminole man hunts gar fish in the backwaters of Florida from a sturdy canoe. An able fisherman can snare a fish with a lightning-quick thrust of the spear.

LEFT A Seminole woman poses in a European-style dress and shawl with her baby secured to her back. Because of the Seminole policy to welcome runaway slaves from both the Southern states and the Caribbean, and adopt them into their villages, a number of those in the Native American and African cultures intermarried.

THE NATCHEZ

During most of the European-provoked wars on the Indians, the Natchez and Taënsa of Mississippi, descendants of the Mexican-influenced Mississippian culture, lived in relative peace. Then, an expedition down the Mississippi by French explorer René-Robert de la Salle in 1682 brought white men into the region. By the turn of the eighteenth century, the French had established a colony along the Gulf Coast from New Orleans to Mobile. After a 1729 land swindle, the Natchez attacked a French fort and killed 300 colonists. The French and their Choctaw allies waged war against the Natchez; the few survivors were absorbed by sympathetic Chickasaw and Cherokee villages.

ABOVE LEFT This deep buff ware bowl with an unusual flanged rim was discovered at Crystal River in Citrus County, Florida. The area on Florida's west coast has been set aside as a protected archeological park.

ABOVE RIGHT Decoys were used among the tribes of Florida and elsewhere to attract small game. Using bark, feathers, and other materials they were practical handicraft projects for members of a number of tribes. This one, made of painted tule reeds and feathers, was discovered in Lovelock Cave, Nevada.

ABOVE A drawing of Fort Caroline on Florida's St. John's River as seen from above. Fort Caroline was an attempt to establish a foothold in an area of Spanish domination. In 1564 Rene de Laudonniere built the fort with 200 French colonists. A year later the Spanish king sent Pedro Menéndez de Avilés to attack the reinforced fort but the assault failed. Menéndez sailed 40 miles (64 km) south, built Fort Augustine, then attacked Fort Caroline again, killing 132 colonists and driving the French from the region. He renamed the place Fort San Mateo and continued establishing forts to the north to win Native American peace and Catholic converts.

THE FRENCH & INDIAN WAR

JOIN, or DIE.

THE FRENCH AND INDIAN WAR IS THE NAME GIVEN TO THE FINAL STRUGGLE FOR CONTROL OF NORTH AMERICA THAT DECIDED WHETHER FRANCE OR BRITAIN WOULD CONTROL THE EASTERN PART OF THE CONTINENT. IT WAS THE CULMINATION OF A SERIES OF CONFLICTS FOUGHT IN BOTH THE OLD AND NEW WORLDS.

France, with power in the hands of King Louis XV and his advisors, and Britain, with power shared between King George II and its constitutional government, dominated European politics. Their economic might and military and naval strength enabled them to colonize many parts of the world. Although there had been conflicts and treaties affecting North America before 1754, these were incidental to the global balance of power. The greatest change previously was that in 1713 a treaty transferred a large part of Nova Scotia to Britain from New France, the French colony that stretched from eastern Canada to the Great Lakes.

ABOVE Benjamin Franklin created this eighteeenth-century political cartoon in his *Pennsylvania Gazette* on May 9, 1754. The woodcut accompanied an essay Franklin wrote urging unity among the bitterly divided colonies as the only way to assure that dangers from the French and their allies could be countered effectively. Franklin's overall political thinking was greatly influenced by the Iroquois leader Canassatego, who spoke at an Indian–British assembly in Philadelphia in 1744.

LEFT The defeat of a combined force of Indians, colonists, and British regulars under General Edward Braddock along the Monongahela River, July 9, 1755, on the approach to Fort Duquesne, was a tragic case of a leader ill-fitted to the role. Though possessing unquestionable personal bravery, Braddock's disdain for his Native American and colonial allies, and his failure to adapt to wilderness fighting, caused needless loss of life as well as the campaign.

What was at stake in North America was trade with Native Americans. Even though these European powers derived more income from Caribbean sugar operations than from furs, tobacco, and other products imported from North America, the balance of power across the large continent was crucial to each empire. Key to success were the ties maintained with the Indian tribes with which they traded. The French had the advantage of starting earlier and establishing a network of modest posts and a few forts throughout the vast north and western regions, such as at Fort Detroit (1701). With these they carried on the necessary commerce while posing no great threat to the Indians' homes and hunting grounds. The British provided the tribes with better quality and cheaper trade goods, but the constant flow of more settlers inland in the semi-autonomous colonies was of greater concern to the Indians.

War finally came to a head over a previously underutilized portion of the continent, the Ohio Valley. When English traders pushed west of the Appalachians in the 1750s and discovered the network of rivers that fed the Ohio, they began to trade in the region, controlled by the powerful Iroquois alliance. Plans were made to build forts and settle the area. The French saw this as a threat to their vast trade network, from the Great Lakes region down the Mississippi Valley to New Orleans. The governor of New France was ordered to drive the British traders out. Both sides met with the tribes of the Ohio Valley to seek allies. The British made efforts to unite the separate colonies, form militia units, import regular soldiers, and firm up Indian alliances.

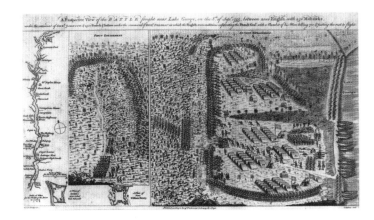

ABOVE A woodcut diagram of the Battle of Lake George, fought near Lake George on September 8, 1755. Colonial troops and Native Americans under the British colonies' premier Indian agent, General William Johnson, defeated a force of French regulars, Canadians, and Indians under Jean-Armand Dieskau, the supreme French commander in Canada at the time.

A fort was built by the British on a triangle of land where the Allegheny and Monongahela Rivers joined to form the Ohio, the gateway to the region. The war started in June 1754, when a young Virginia militia commander, George Washington, led a force with orders from the Governor of Virginia to retake the fort, which the French had seized. Washington's men, accompanied by Native American allies, fired on a French patrol, killing the commander. The incident led to a larger French force surrounding Washington's camp, called Fort Necessity, and then forcing the Virginians to surrender. Washington and most

SCARAOUADY

Scaraouady was an Oneida chief who remained unwavering in his support of the British during the war. He had control of members of the Iroquois Confederacy and other tribes in the upper Ohio Valley, the most strategic and contested area in the French and Indian War. Initially Scaraouady was interested in keeping the French from the area, but also opposed the building of a British fort there. He met with George Washington on a peace mission in November 1753 and fought beside him in the first skirmish of the war. Later, he was at the side of General Edward Braddock in the disastrous defeat on the Monongahela River which led to the general's mortal wounding (pictured left). Scaraouady was well-spoken and frequently addressed the colonial governments.

ABOVE In this engraving of a dramatic painting by Felix Octavius Carr Darley, the Marquis de Montcalm, the French general in command in Canada, is shown trying to stop Native Americans from attacking unarmed British and colonial soldiers leaving Fort William Henry in August 1757. Montcalm gave the defenders generous surrender terms, disappointing his Abnaki allies as he tried to prevent the eventual killing of nearly 200.

of his force were allowed to return Virginia, with Washington reporting to the governor in Williamsburg.

From this modest beginning, the two sides prepared for a major conflict. Britain's strong-willed Prime Minister, William Pitt, pushed for complete victory in America and mobilized a huge war effort. British regulars backed by artillery, colonial militia, and warriors from the Mohawk, Catawba, Creek, and Cherokee tribes faced off against French and Canadian forces and their Indian allies from the Catholicized Iroquois of Canada and Great Lakes tribes. The war was fought on two fronts, with a combination of sieges, formal battles, and guerrilla-style combat waged by small patrols in the undeveloped frontier. Both sides scored victories, with the British taking of Fort Duquesne (Pittsburgh) in 1758, Fort Niagara and Quebec in 1759, and Montreal (1760), proving more decisive than French victories at Monongahela, Fort Oswego (1756), Fort William Henry (1757), and elsewhere.

In the end, with greater numbers of soldiers and a superior navy able to transport men and materiel across the Atlantic freely, while also blockading New France's resupply along their main water artery, the St. Lawrence River, the British won the war. The final peace treaty, signed in 1763, handed control over Canada to the British. Although not the only war fought between whites for colonial interests in which Native Americans participated, it was perhaps the one in which they fought in greatest numbers on both sides. One of the war's most devastating consequences for them was seeing the victor gain more of their land through increased post-war settlement between the Appalachian Mountains and the Mississippi River.

ABOVE The death of General Wolfe in the Battle of Quebec, September 1759. Though he found a way to overcome Quebec's strong natural defensive cliffs by funneling troops up a narrow path and onto the Plains of Abraham adjacent to Quebec's undefended west, General James Wolfe might have missed the chance for victory had not Louis Jordan, the Marquis de Montcalm, sent a fraction of his command outside Quebec's fortifications to meet him. The resulting battle caused the deaths of both commanders and the beginning of the end for the French and their Indian allies in the war.

ABOVE RIGHT The *American Magazine*, published in Philadelphia, displayed on the cover of its March 1758 issue a woodcut of a Frenchman and an Englishman competing for the loyalty of a Native American standing between them leaning on a rifle. Praevalebit Aequior, meaning "The appropriate one will prevail," refers to the gift-giving that accompanied the recruitment of braves to fight for one side or the other.

ABOVE LEFT A novel wooden-handled pipe tomahawk.

TOMAHAWK

The tomahawk was probably the Native American weapon most feared during the French and Indian War. In the hands of a skilled warrior it could club or bash open the head of a victim or if thrown a short distance it could slice open a large gash. Originally tomahawks comprised a stone head, grooved in the middle and tied with hide strips to a notched stick. Under European influence, the stone heads were often replaced by pounded and sharpened metal. Some metal heads were bored out, and the implement doubled as a smoking receptacle, giving rise to the term "pipe tomahawk."

RIGHT Several tomahawk styles are displayed here. A leather wrapped stone makes the head of one, while pounded metal tops the other. Both are mounted on wooden handles.

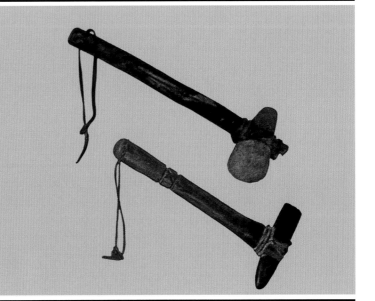

By the HONOURABLE

SPENCER PHIPS, Esq;

Lieutenant-Governour and Commander in Chief for the Time being of His Majesty's Province of the *Massachusetts-Bay* in *New-England.*

A *PROCLAMATION* for Encouragement to Voluntiers to prosecute the WAR against the *Indian Enemy.*

HEREAS the Indians of the *Penobscot* and *Norridgewack* Tribes, and other Eastern Indians, as also the Indians inhabiting the *French* Territories, and Parts adjacent thereto, have by their Violation of their solemn Treaties, and by open Hostilities committed against His Majesty's Subjects of this Province, oblig'd Me, with the Advice of His Majesty's Council, to declare War against them ;

And whereas the General Assembly in their late Session, have *Voted* " For the Encouragement of any
" Company, Party, or Person singly, of His Majesty's Subjects belonging to and residing within this Province, who shall vo-
" luntarily, and at their own proper Cost and Charge, go out and kill a Male Indian of the Age of twelve Years or upwards
" of such Eastern Indians, or such others as may be found with them at any Time so long as the War may continue, and
" produce the Scalp in Evidence of his Death, the Sum of *One hundred Pounds*, in Bills of Credit on this Province of the new
" Tenor ; and the Sum of *One hundred and five Pounds* in said Bills for any Male of like Age who shall be taken Captive,
" and deliver'd to the Order of the Captain General, to be at the Disposal and for the Use of the Government ; and the Sum
" of *Fifty Pounds* in said Bills for each Woman, and the like Sum for Children under the Age of twelve Years kill'd in Fight,
" and *Fifty five Pounds* in said Bills for such when taken Prisoners, and the Plunder ; And to such Person or Persons of this
" Province as aforesaid, for whom the Province shall provide Ammunition and Provisions, *viz.* Provisions from the Day
" they go forth until their Return, to be paid in said Bills for each Male above the Age of twelve Years, kill'd, and Scalp pro-
" duc'd, the Sum of *Seventy five Pounds*, and Captives *Seventy eight Pounds fifteen Shillings* ; and for a Female and Others
" as aforesaid, kill'd, and Scalp produc'd, *Thirty seven Pounds ten Shillings*, and Captives *Thirty nine Pounds five Shillings* ;
" And to the Inhabitants of this Province, and such Soldiers as may be employed by the Province, who shall issue out upon
" any Party or Parties of Indians, for each Male above twelve Years, kill'd, and Scalp produc'd as aforesaid, *Thirty Pounds*,
" and for a Captive *Thirty three Pounds* like Bills, for a Female and Others kill'd, and Scalp produc'd, *Fifteen Pounds*, and
" Captives of the like Sort *Sixteen Pounds ten Shillings* ; And that the like Premium be given for any Indian kill'd, and Scalp
" produc'd, as aforesaid, or Captive taken, who shall be found arm'd (unless call'd in to our Aid) easterly of a Line drawn
" from the *Massachusetts* Block-House near *Hoosuck* over to *Crown-Point*, *viz.* between such a Line and the eastern Fron-
" tiers of this Province and *New-Hampshire*. Provided no Payment be made as aforesaid for killing and captivating any
" Indian as aforesaid, until Proof be made to the Acceptance of the Governour and Council. "

I have therefore thought fit, with the Advice of His Majesty's Council, to issue this Proclamation,
for giving publick Notice of the Encouragement granted by the General-Court to all Persons who
may be disposed to serve their King and Country against the Indians aforesaid ; as also to inform
all Persons concerned, That the several Premiums which were granted for a certain Term (now
expired) for the killing and captivating the Indians of the St. Johns and Cape-Sables Tribes, are now
granted a-new by the General Court for one Year, or such Term of Time as the War shall continue
with the said Indians.

Given at the Council Chamber in *Boston*, the *Twenty-third* Day of *August*, 1745. In the Nineteenth Year of the Reign of our
Sovereign Lord GEORGE the Second, by the Grace of GOD of *Great-Britain*, *France* and *Ireland*, KING, Defender
of the Faith, &c.

By Order of the Honourable the
Lieutenant Governour, with
the Advice of the Council,
    J. Willard, *Secr.*

S. PHIPS.

GOD save the KING.

BOSTON: Printed by *John Draper*, Printer to His Excellency the GOVERNOUR and COUNCIL.

An Acco.t of Peltry bo.t at the Province Store from y.e 2.d April 1763 to y.e 28.th may follow.g Fort Pitt 1764

1763	Fall Skins	Summer	Bears	Panthers	Elks	Otters	Cats	Foxes	Fishers	Wolves	Martins	Beaver	Castor W.t	Racoons	Sm.ll Cub.ff	Muskrats	Wezel	W.t Raff.ff	W.t Beaver	W.t Summer	W.t Fall	Cost
April 3	23	4	2	1	2	.	18	43	2	.	.	1	5¼	43	.	2	.	.	2	12½	104	£ 20. 0. 11
14	6	1	.	2	.	.	.	.	.	.	71	.	7	.	.	.	.	1.	123	5	24½	29. 11. 5
26	.	.	.	.	.	.	.	.	.	.	4	.	.	.	.	.	.	.	7½	.	.	2. 3. —
may 10	1	.	4	.	1	3	2	1	.	.	47	.	10	.	.	.	.	.	29	.	3	11. 18. 6
20	15	.	23	1	3	.	5	12	2	.	6	.	13	.	.	.	.	.	11	.	70	16. 12. 6
	6	.	3	.	.	1	.	.	.	.	47	.	39	1	.	.	.	¾	93	.	24	33. 1. 3
22	1	.	7	.	.	.	.	2	1	.	13	.	3	.	.	.	.	.	28	.	5	11. 18. —
25	2	.	3	.	.	1	.	.	1	.	10	.	20	.	.	.	.	.	23½	.	10	9. 18. —
26	26	1	2	1	.	4	3	1	2	.	59	.	63	.	.	.	.	.	109	2	129	53. 10. 11
27	.	.	.	2	.	.	.	.	.	.	.	.	.	.	.	.	.	.	.	.	.	. 15
	73	.	.	.	.	1	4	.	.	.	43	.	22	.	.	.	.	.	74	.	346	53. 4. 6
	.	1	2	.	.	.	2	1	.	1	3	.	15	.	.	.	.	.	4	4	.	3. 14. 0
	47	.	5	.	.	2	13	.	.	1	14	.	79	.	1	.	.	.	25	.	228	34. 2. 9
	.	.	5	.	.	2	.	.	.	.	34	3½	3	.	.	.	.	.	63	.	.	23. 3. 6
																						£ 323. 14. 3

N.B. 28 Bear Skins & 5 Fall Skins were Sold out of this for £ 8. 10. 0 — & the Elks were Cut up for Ropes. the Bears for Wrappers. ——

[signature: Cm. ... / ... Davenport Agent]

FUR PELT ACCOUNT

At the end of the war, the confluence of the Allegheny, Monongahela, and Ohio rivers became an important commerce center, and the British established Fort Pitt on the site of Fort Duquesne, which the French had destroyed. This ledger lists pelts (animal furs) traded by Indians at Fort Pitt in 1764. A number of animal skin types are listed across the top of the ledger, representative of the popular trade varieties. Pelts were usually exchanged for finished goods, such as tools, guns, and clothing.

MASSACHUSETTS PROCLAMATION (OPPOSITE)

In the wars involving colonial expansion prior to the Seven Years' War, better known as the French and Indian War, the British colonies were virtually left to fend for themselves. This proclamation by the Lieutenant Governor of Massachusetts, issued on August 23, 1745 during the conflict known as King George's War, calls for colonists to hunt down Indians and offers a bounty for proof of a kill or capture. This desperate action was in reaction to French-sanctioned raids by their Indian allies on the New England colonies.

THE CALIFORNIA MISSION SYSTEM

WEST OF THE HOHOKAM AND MOGOLLÓN WERE MEMBERS
OF THE DESERT TRADITION THAT DID NOT EXPERIENCE THE
EXTREMES OF CLIMATIC CONDITIONS ENDURED BY THEIR
NEIGHBORS TO THE EAST. YET THEY PRACTICED NO AGRICULTURE,
FOR THEIR PLANT-BASED DIETS CAME FROM GATHERING.

They are known as the Acorn People and until less than a century ago, similar primitive societies still existed in parts of Baja California. The Acorn People of Alta California lived primarily along the coast, from the current United States border with Mexico to the San Francisco Bay area, where a somewhat different culture began to appear.

The Acorn People did not subsist solely on the hard nuts of oak trees lining inland canyons and foothills, but it was the basis of a meal from which they derived their basic calorific needs. The potentially deadly tannic acid that prevents acorns from being a modern food was leached out after grinding. To supplement this staple, people gathered other wild grasses and roots, as well as insects, hunted deer and rabbit, and netted fish and clams. They lived in conical thatched grass houses, but spent most of the mild-weather months shielded by a reed roof supported by wooden poles. They wore very little clothing, made baskets and other woven utensils, and had simple belief systems. Their most involved ceremonies were the coming-of-age rituals. Of all these tribes, the Chumash were the only ones to exploit the sea fully, using crafted plank boats to navigate the island channels off the coast of their homeland near present-day Malibu, Ventura, and Santa Barbara.

The tribes of the Acorn People lived their lives unchanged in California for thousands of years. Then, in 1769, in an effort to expand their colonial power, the Spanish sent an expedition

LEFT J. Ed Bacon of Salinas photographed Old Gabriel, a Monterey Indian, about the turn of the twentieth century. His notes list the man as being 145 years old at the time and that he helped build the Carmel Mission. Construction for Mission San Carlos Borromeo de Carmelo was begun in 1770 and improvements would have gone on for years, so the claim may have merit.

north to Alta California. Led by Father Junipero Serra, the Franciscan friars, backed by soldiers, began to establish missions. The first was Mission San Diego de Alcalá, and then San Carlos Borromeo, San Antonio de Padua, San Gabriel (near modern Los Angeles), and San Luis Obispo (in 1772). The missions' purpose was to convert the natives to Christianity, and so the friars, aided by soldiers based in presidios (forts) nearby, drove the Indians from their homes and into the missions.

These Native Americans then underwent a transformation, both physically and spiritually. They were dressed in Spanish-inspired cotton attire, were taught to farm and make pottery, and, of course, instructed in the rigid religious beliefs of the Franciscans. Previously married couples were allowed to share

FROM TRIBES TO BANDS

The transition of California's southern and central coast Indians from an independent lifestyle to the highly structured and disciplined life of the missions and back again was a shock to their cultures. Many died from European diseases to which they had no resistance, and the survivors suffered from the scattering of their population after secularization. Those that remained as communities sought refuge in the inland areas away from the rancheros and coastal developments. There they formed bands, practiced the agricultural techniques learned at the missions, and continued to produce outstanding basketry.

RIGHT Mission San Diego de Alcalá. This was the first mission founded in Alta California by Father Junipero Serra and was begun on July 16, 1769, at the Presidio overlooking San Diego Bay. The pictured mission building is the chapel of the second mission, built six miles (10 km) inland in 1774. It was used as a mission, military barracks, and church, and fell into great disrepair by the time of this 1904 photograph. A major reconstruction was begun in 1931.

BELOW RIGHT A late-eighteenth-century illustration shows Native Americans and Catholic padres working together to build an unidentified mission. Missions continued to be built in isolated areas after secularization, as those Mission Indians who had undergone transformation were attracted to subsequent missionary ventures by a handful of friars.

small huts, but the rest of the tribe's people were segregated by sexes and occupied dormitory-style buildings. The missions were set up around an open courtyard and most daily activities—prayer, instruction, meals, and some of the work—were carried out within the courtyard. Continued building expanded the compounds, and eventually most contained an outer wall.

The Indians were well treated but discipline was harsh. Some individuals escaped, but with their villages destroyed by the soldiers, they had nowhere to go, and a number of those who fled returned to the missions. Gradually, over the next 50 years, the mission system grew to include 21 separate missions, with the last, San Francisco Solano, built at Sonoma and completed in 1823, to stem the tide of Russian influence flowing down from the north. Although there were cases of violence, such as a massacre of Franciscans by rebellious Indians at Mission San Diego de Alcalá (on November 5, 1775), most of the members of the Mission Indian tribes just endured the strict mission life and some actually benefited from their experiences.

SECULARIZATION AND EMANCIPATION

In 1834, the California missions were secularized by the newly independent Mexican government. Unsure of the loyalty of the powerful Franciscans in Alta California and sensitive to pressure from the owners of huge ranches there, the secularization reduced the church's political clout. The Mission Indians were freed from the control of the friars. Since many had been born and raised on the missions, the adjustment to freedom was a profound shock. Many ended up in indentured servitude on the ranches, but others who did not formed into communities again. The Emancipation Proclamation of California Tribes was a unified statement that reaffirmed the freedom of the Acorn People's descendants.

THE CALIFORNIAN MISSION SYSTEM

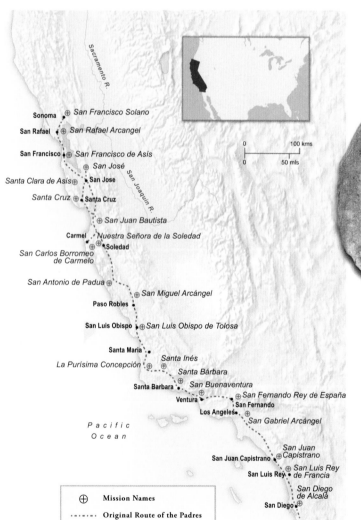

BELOW A Chumash metate (grinding surface) and mano (muller). A Chumash woman would roll the metate over the mano to produce corn meal.

ABOVE Petroglyphs at Sloan Canyon, Nevada. A trove of intricate petroglyphs by people of the Desert Tradition was discovered at Sloan Canyon in the southern Nevada desert in the early twentieth century.

BOTTOM Chumash pictographs in the mountains of Malibu, California, tell the tale in pictures of the journey of Don Gaspár de Portolá through the area in November 1769.

EMANCIPATION PROCLAMATION

The Emancipation Proclamation of California Tribes was an 1833 document in Spanish that outlined the process by which the former Mission Indians were to receive the distribution of land, livestock, and seed to begin their lives outside the mission complex. It was originally conceived by the Mexican Governor for Alta California, José Figueroa, but he died in 1835 and subsequent politicians and Mexican ranchers cheated many of the emancipated Indians and gained titles to their land grants. See Translations, page 157.

del supremo Govierno y Exma. Diputacion Territorial se observen por ahora las prevenciones siguientes.

1ª El Gefe Politico determinará el numero de individuos que se hande emancipar en cada Mision, y el tiempo en que se hade verificar. Nombrará á los comisionados que juzgue á proposito para la ejecucion de estas prevenciones.

2ª Serán emancipados, los que tengan mas de doce años de cristianos reducidos, que sean casados, ó viudos con hijos: que sepan cultivar la tierra ó ejerzan algun oficio, y que tengan aplicacion al travajo. La calificacion se hara por los comisionados que nombre el Gefe Politico asociado delos Ministros respectivos de cada Mision.

3ª Los que se emancipen quedan subordinados á las autoridades respectivas y á los RR.PP. Ministros delas Misiones que ejerzan con ellos las funciones x Parrocos en todo lo concerniente á la administraccion Espiritual.

4ª A los que se emancipen se les acudirá *durante un año* con las semillas para sus primeras siembras y con la racion que se acostumbra daales p. su subsistencia en la Mision á que pertenezcan, y ellos estarán obligados por el mismo tiempo, á concurrir con su travajo personal en auxilio de la Mision quando se hagan las siembras y cosechas, y en una u otra faena que necesite de sus brazos, quedando á la prudencia del Ministro misionero y del Alcalde el

ó sacar madera, formar presas, corrales y rodeos: construir casas consistoriales, Yglesia, carcel, y demas obras que vayan necesitando: cubiran las lineas divisorias delos linderos delas suertes de tierra con arboles frutales u otros de alguna utilidad que sirvan de mohonera y de cerco.

22ª El terreno que por muerte del propietario y sus herederos quedare baldio, buelve á poder dela Nacion.

23ª Los emancipados que desatendieren sus labores y ganados, ó que los dirijen y no cultiven sus terrenos y f abandonen sus casas para bagar indistintamente entregados á la olgazaneria y vicios, serán sometidos nuevamente á la mision de donde salieron previa calificac.ª del Alcalde y parroco, quienes antes de proceder con cada el que incurriese le amonestarán por dos veces á que enmiende su conducta dandole tiempo suficiente para que acredite su comportamiento.

24ª Las autoridades cuidarán del exacto cumplimiento de estas prevenciones, y seran responzables de las infracciones si saviendolo no pusieran remedio.

San Diego Julio 15 de 1833.

José Figueroa

RUSSIAN INFLUENCE IN THE NORTHWEST

THE ESKIMOS, ALEUTS, AND OTHER TRIBES OF THE ARCTIC
AND SUB-ARCTIC REGIONS OF NORTH AMERICA WERE
THE LAST TO EMIGRATE FROM ASIA, BUT SOME OF THEM
WERE THE VERY FIRST TO ENCOUNTER EUROPEANS.

In late tenth century, on the icy coast of Greenland, a Norseman named Erik the Red led an expedition across the Northern Atlantic and founded the first European settlement in the New World. A few Norsemen made it as far west as Labrador. The colony and the Eskimos who inhabited the region had little to do with each other. Then in the twelfth century, the climate became colder, more Eskimos migrated to the region, and the Norse colonists either died, were murdered, or were absorbed into the native tribes. Virtually no trace of their journey to the sub-continent of Greenland exists save some written records and recent archeological finds. It would be another 300 years before the Greenlanders and the rest of the Eskimos' fascinating culture would be disturbed by the white man's influence.

To the Eskimos that inhabited the region near and beyond the Arctic Circle, the harsh climate was something that required only slight adaptation from the life in their assumed original

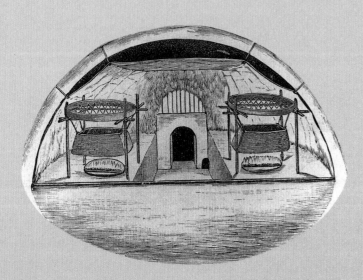

ABOVE Diagram of an igloo interior. As observed by Admiral Robert Peary and other visitors to Arctic areas, igloos were well designed to withstand the extreme climate. Several vestibules provided for temperature zones between the entrance and living area, and larger igloos had separate rooms for storage and living space for the dogs.

ABOVE Mrs. Kleinschmidt, the wife of the photographer, was a dinner guest of the Eskimo family inside their igloo in this 1913 photograph. They all wore traditional dress and dined on frozen crabs. Among the family's possessions visible in the picture are snow shoes and a coiled rope.

ABOVE A summer sealskin tent with an old Eskimo woman sitting outside at Point Barrow, Alaska. These dwellings were constructed for the short summer season, anchored on poles of willow or driftwood and held down against strong winds by rocks.

THE IGLOO

Another Eskimo invention was the igloo, or ice house. These domed habitats were constructed of packed snow bricks, carefully built up for integral support, and placed on frozen ice flows for temporary or long-term winter shelter. More permanent styles could contain several interconnected rooms and storage areas. Windows were made from ice sheets or seal innards, and an exhaust hole in the top carried away fumes and smoke. With a frozen condensation layer formed by the temperature difference, the occupants could be quite comfortable inside with little or no clothing. In the summer, seal-skin tents replaced the igloos for shelter. A skilled Eskimo could construct a temporary igloo on the hunt in less than an hour.

homeland of Siberia a mere 3,000 years earlier. Along with the Aleuts and the inland Eyak, they ranged across approximately the upper third of the continent. Their language base in the west was Athapaskan, in the east, Algonquian. Their diet was, with few exceptions, totally carnivorous, and traditionally hunting was the main occupation for males, with some assistance from the women. The game for the inland Eyak tribes included the mammals that roamed the tundra; bears, moose, oxen, and, most importantly, caribou. Migrating birds in the summer and fish supplemented their diet and provided for many other needs. The Aleuts, living on the wooded islands that once formed the land bridge, hunted smaller mammals, game birds, and fish, netted or snared with lines and hooks.

Along coastal Alaska and the Arctic areas of northwestern Canada, whaling was also practiced, not just as a symbol of male prowess—on which the Nootka set great store—but as a source of food, oil, clothing, and construction materials. The whales, primarily beluga and white, were tracked by teams in open boats called umiaks, then harpooned and speared as the animals tired. Sometimes whales could be caught while breeding in inlet waters.

The Eskimos, who inhabited the upper reaches of Canada and Alaska, had one predominant prey, the seal. Of tantamount importance to their survival was seal oil, which, when burned in stone bowls, provided light and warmth in a land almost totally devoid of any kind of timber. Just as the Plains Indians used virtually every part of the bison, so too the Eskimos found practical uses for every bit of the seal's body. In a culture without organized religion, the Eskimos would perform a ritual after killing to release the animal's spirit.

ABOVE This kayak equipped for seal hunting belonged to an Eskimo from Nunivak Island, Alaska. Among the hunting items shown are harpoons and a float made from seal intestines.

ABOVE This photograph shows the process of drying salmon at the Aleut village of Old Harbor, Alaska, in 1889. The relatively mild climate of the Aleutian Islands afforded the natives a wider range of fish species for food to augment plant foods, birds, seals, and other mammals.

When European influence returned to the region, it was at first fully exploitative, and later a dash of paternalism was added to the exploitation. Russian traders came to Alaska and the west coast in search of ivory and fur between 1740 and 1765. The Tsar of Russia stepped in toward the end of the eighteenth century and required chartered fur and whaling companies to bring Orthodox missionaries to the New World as an obligatory part of their teams. Churches and schools became common in the Aleutian Islands and many converts were counted among those who survived the diseases introduced by the foreigners. On the Alaskan mainland, the missionaries met with more resistance. From the other direction, the Hudson's Bay Company, which had a virtual monopoly over the fur trade throughout most of Canada and beyond, quickly realized the practicality of looking after its Native American trappers with education and other social programs. As Canada formed a more independent government, these commercial efforts were replaced by provincial programs, and peace and order were brought to a lawless area with the establishment of the Royal Canadian Mounted Police in 1873.

LEFT This harpoon and tether is attributed to the Clayquot tribe of the west coast of Vancouver Island, British Columbia. The point is made of antler.

THE KAYAK

The kayak, a skin-covered sleek watercraft, was an Eskimo invention, which neighboring tribes adapted. The true Eskimo kayak was pointed at bow and stern, made of cured sealskin stretched on a whalebone or driftwood frame, and ranged in size up to the most common, 18 feet (5.5 metres). It was a one-man boat. With clothing attached to the small round opening amidships, the complete package was watertight. Capsizing was not a problem and the craft could be easily righted with the double-ended paddle—another Eskimo invention—used to propel the kayak.

BELOW A Tlingit fishing camp of wooden A-frame huts at Lituya Bay, Alaska, is pictured in this 1786 engraving. The village, called Port of France by the French naval officer who sketched it, was established by the inhabitants for the fishing season.

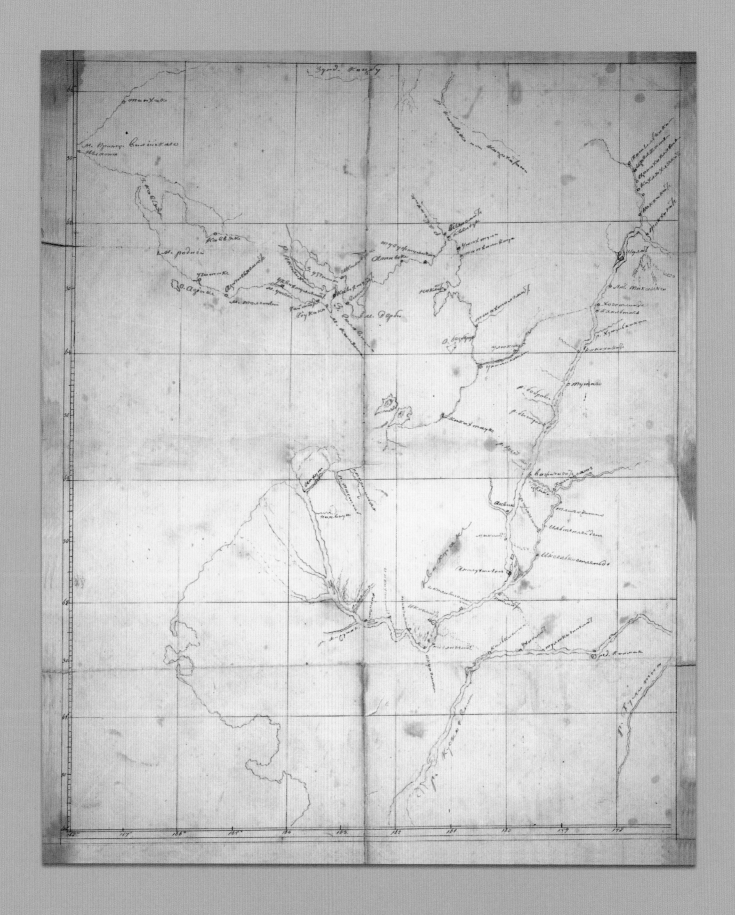

ИГА́ЛУТЪ АТХ҃ИТЪ ТАММА́ЙТНИ ШУГНИ:
НАЗВА́НІЕ МѢСЯЦОВЪ ПО ОБЩЕПРИНЯТОМУ:

Анꙋ́лакъ	Январь
Унꙋ́лалакъ	Февраль
Ма́лтакъ	Мартъ
Аплилакъ	Апрѣль
Ма́акъ	Май
Ию́накъ	Іюнь
Июлакъ	Іюль
Аꙋгꙋ́штакъ	Августъ
Шинта́плакъ	Сентябрь
Ꙋкта́плакъ	Октябрь
Нꙋа́плакъ	Ноябрь
Дика́плакъ.	Декабрь.

НА҃КИЧИКЪ.

Аганꙋн-Хла́къ	Вивтаг-мюа́ни	Тама-Хла́къ	Лима-мюа́ни
А	Алхилꙋ́къ	1	I
В	Малгꙋ́къ	2	II
Г	Пинга́юнъ	3	III
Д	Чта́манъ	4	IV
Е	Та́лиманъ	5	V
Ѕ	Агꙋ́нлгынъ	6	VI
З	Малхꙋ́нгинъ	7	VII
И	Инлꙋ́лгынъ	8	VIII
Ѳ	Кꙋлнгꙋ́анъ	9	IX
І	Кꙋ́лынъ	10	X
АІ	Атхахтꙋ́нъ	11	XI

PRIEST'S MAP (OPPOSITE)

A map of the Russian Orthodox priest Father Iakov Netsvetov's travels through the Alaskan interior from 1828–43 accompanied a journal of his experiences. The large river extending to the upper right corner of the map, along which he denotes the location of many villages, is the Yukon River. Although the large river shown can be identified through geographic features as the Yukon River, and the large body of water at the left center of the map as today's Norton Bay, none of the places named on the map—all in new Russian—have survived as names of modern villages, towns or geographical landmarks.

ALEUT PRIMERS

Russian Aleut Primer. The Russian Church in America strove to retain native languages and use them to communicate their religious teachings. Father Ioann Veniaminov created an alphabet for the Aleut language, and aided by the Aleut Toien (Chief), who went by the name Ivan Pan'kov, wrote an Aleut catechism in 1834 and this primer in 1845. See Translations, page 156.

THE NEW NATION &
THE ORIGINAL INHABITANTS

AFTER THE UNITED STATES GAINED ITS INDEPENDENCE FROM GREAT BRITAIN, THE GOVERNING BODIES OF THE NEW NATION TURNED THEIR ATTENTION TO OTHER SOURCES OF CONFLICT. THESE WERE DOMESTIC ISSUES BROUGHT ON BY THE WESTWARD EXPANSION OF WHITE SETTLEMENTS.

King George III had declared the Appalachian Mountains to be the boundary of the colonies, while the land to the west was considered the sovereign territory of the Native American tribes. However, long before Cornwallis met with defeat at Yorktown in 1781, white settlers were pressing beyond that frontier and carving out farms on Indian land. Though some eastern and southeast tribes fought for the American Revolution—including members of the Oneida, Tuscarora, and Cauhnawaga tribes who fought with the Continental Army at Saratoga—many Native Americans viewed the United States and its infant government with distrust, even hostility.

The new federal government adopted a policy of pacification in its relations with the Native Americans. George Washington's administration set up government trading houses, in Washington's words, to "conciliate the Indians' attachment." It was more of a political maneuver rather than an economic one. The idea was to keep the tribes as small independent entities under the protection of the federal government. In 1786, the Treaty of Hopewell between the federal government and the Cherokees, Choctaws, and Chickasaws set boundaries for Indian lands and established laws to protect Indian sovereignty. But encroachment by settlers continued.

Native American animosity toward the government increased in the region affected by the Northwest Ordinance of 1787, which created the Northwest Territory, and established a procedure by which states could be created out of the western settlements. The tribes in what are now Ohio, Indiana, Illinois,

Wisconsin, and Michigan preferred British and French trappers and trading companies over the frontier farmers of the United States. The white settlers' approach to the Native Americans was generally one of lawlessness. Tribal settlements and individual Indians were treated roughly or violently. In 1791, Native Americans armed by British individuals attacked settlements in the Northwest Territories, and a group of U.S. soldiers was attacked and scattered near the Wabash River in Ohio.

ABOVE LEFT Though he himself was a Shawnee chief, Billy Shane fought against his tribesmen who were aligned with the British in the War of 1812. He was wounded in the Battle of Thames, Ontario, Canada.

ABOVE RIGHT By the time George Washington became the first American president, he had already dealt with Native Americans as a military commander in two wars. He took cautious control of Indian affairs in the new nation through trade, treaties, and military action.

TECUMSEH

Tecumseh, the dynamic chief of the Shawnee tribe, had fought—like his eventual foe William Henry Harrison—in the Battle of Fallen Timbers. In November 1811, Harrison moved against a village on Tippecanoe Creek controlled by Tecumseh's brother Tenskwatawa, known as The Prophet. Tecumseh then organized woodland tribes against the American settlers and aligned the confederation he had formed with the British in the War of 1812. After Tecumseh's death at the Battle of Thames in 1813, no other chief could fill the void left by the loss of the charismatic leader.

BELOW In the Battle of Thames, at Malden, Ontario October 5, 1813, the 2,500 Kentucky militia and 200 U.S. Regulars advanced on British troops and Tecumseh's warriors. Oliver Hazard Perry's victory over the British Navy on Lake Erie imperiled British control of southern Ontario, but Tecumseh insisted that the British hold the area. This fanciful nineteenth-century lithograph of the American victory shows the death of Tecumseh and a mounted William Henry Harrison leading a charge.

ABOVE This proclamation dated December 12, 1792, describes an atrocious act of violence perpetrated against a Cherokee village in Georgia, and offers rewards for bringing the offenders to justice. It is an example of Washington's policy of extending federal protection to the Native American tribes as entities within a larger nation. It is signed by the President and Secretary of State Thomas Jefferson.

ABOVE This copper peace medal bearing the likeness of Thomas Jefferson in an 1801 design was given to Powder Face, a Cheyenne chief. These medals were freely given by the U.S. government in conjunction with treaty negotiations. Many of the chiefs painted by the mid-nineteenth-century painters are posed wearing peace medals.

OPPOSITE The meeting of Tecumseh and William Henry Harrison at Vincennes, the capital of Indiana Territory, in 1809 is portrayed in this lithograph. Tecumseh was angered over the Treaty of Fort Wayne, signed by a number of tribes and chiefs, which ceded 2.5 million acres of Ohio and Indiana to the United States. Tecumseh assured Harrison his followers were not at war with the U.S. then left on a journey to spread his message of resistance to the tribes of the southeast.

BLACK HAWK

Black Hawk's uneventful death on an Iowa reservation in 1838 belied his tumultuous life. He was a Sauk war chief who resented the American government, yet also cautioned against bringing on war. In 1831, he was forced to lead his people west across the Mississippi and sign a treaty banning their return. Challenged by young warriors, he led the Sauks back to their former Illinois planting grounds in 1832. Though he won the Battle of Stillman's Run, Black Hawk, failing to receive support from other tribes, lost most of his followers, including those slaughtered at the Battle of Bad Axe River. Captured, Black Hawk was held up as an example to keep the region peaceful.

Washington issued a warning to the Native American tribes in a series of proclamations in 1794. Later that year, on August 20, an army under General Anthony Wayne defeated a force of braves at Fallen Timbers, Ohio, ending resistance in the region for a time. The Treaty of Greenville signed in 1795 with the chiefs of 12 tribes, including the Shawnee, Miami, and Ottawa, ceded most of Ohio to the United States.

Trouble began again in 1799, as settlers began to move into new Mississippi Territory, created a year earlier. As the nineteenth century began, new developments increased the threats posed to the Native American population. The Louisiana Purchase in 1803 more than doubled the territory of the United States. Additional roads and trails, and the invention of the steam engine for rail and water travel, made settlement easier. President Thomas Jefferson recommended that the tribes east of the Mississippi move to new open territory west of the river. Under Chief Justice John Marshall's leadership, the U.S. Supreme Court invalidated the 1763 boundary line established by the British king, George III, and upheld states' claims to Native American lands.

Conflict returned to the Northwest Territory. In 1811, William Henry Harrison, then governor of Indiana Territory, defeated Native Americans at Tippecanoe Creek in the western part of the state. The Northwest Territory tribes then joined the British in the War of 1812 in a confederation led by Shawnee Chief Tecumseh. Harrison led United States soldiers in defeating the British in the Battle of Thames, Ontario, in 1813. Tecumseh was killed in the battle and the Native American confederacy in the northwest collapsed.

Complementing this muscular approach to Indian affairs was a paternalistic side. In 1816, Governor Lewis Cass of Michigan Territory and William Clark, of the future Lewis and Clark expedition, drew up a series of regulations recognizing a moral obligation to care for Native Americans. The result was a framework of dependency that called for programs for the Native American population, while at the same time forcing them off their lands. New treaties signed by the Creeks and Cherokee caused them to forfeit much of their land.

The U.S. government policy of relocation also affected tribes in the Northwest Territories. Though they signed a treaty in 1804 that allowed for coexistence with whites, the Sauk (Sac) and Fox tribes were forced out of Illinois and west of the Mississippi. In 1832, under Chief Black Hawk, the Sauks returned to Illinois to plant crops. Violence erupted and the Black Hawk War ended with a massacre of tribesmen at Bad Axe River in Wisconsin. By 1850, nearly all Native Americans east of the Mississippi were on reservations.

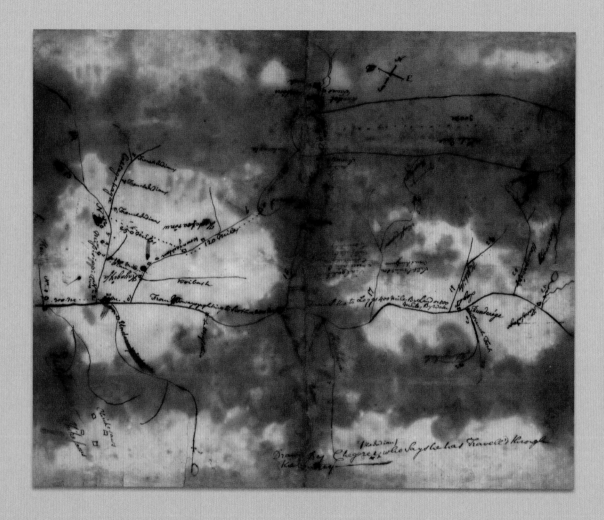
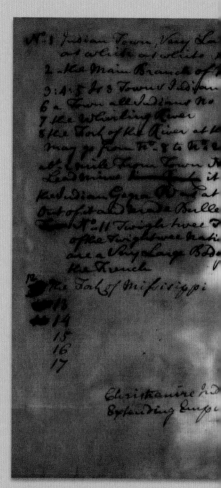

CHEGEREE MAP

THIS mid-eighteenth-century map (above left) of what are now parts of Ohio, Indiana, and neighboring states was created from the accounts of Chegeree, a Native American who claimed to have traveled extensively through the area. It shows Native American villages from Lake Erie to the mouth of the Ohio River where the new American frontier challenged the Indians after the United States gained its independence. The Ohio River was drawn as being straighter than its natural course in maps of this era. The caption at the bottom indicates the map was drawn by Chegeree, but in fact it was done in conjunction with British compatriots who were very interested in the French and their allies in the region. The British had just begun to

explore the region and there was competition with the French. To that end, mention is made of a lead mine and of bullets that were made there. This and other information is in a sidebar (above center), with numbers relating to locations on the map. Another side bar (opposite) asks a number of questions, mostly about distances and navigable waters. Distances between important places are given on the map. The Mississippi River and the Waibash (Wabash) River are identified on the left side of the map, as is the confluence of the Ohio and Mississippi rivers. The only Indian tribe names identified that are generally recognizable are the Chickasaws, villages noted in the lower left portion, and Lower Shawnas (Shawnee) Town, in the map's center.

— 200 Fighting men almost
— True friend to the French
— ippi abt 2 miles over
— ch abt 600 Fighting men
— French Interest abt 200 Warriors

— ar 1/4 mile over — Large Shallow
— the Creek Westward is a Large
— ge Rock of Ore as Big as a horse
— Warriors 4 Days & Melted Lead

— from No 11 to No 10 — are 6 Towns
— in amity with one another they
— ople and hold in friendship with

Over at the Fork

their friendship — Trade

Quere — How far is it from Twightwee Town No 11 to the Fork
of Miss.e Erie No 9 —

What Land is it Between the Two places

What Climate at Twightwee Town No 11

how far is it from Twightwee Town No 11 to Lake Erie

Is it navigable all the Way from Twightwee Town No 11
to Lake Erie & for what Sort of Vessel,

how far is it from Twightwee Town No 11 to Wowayou-
tan river where its navigable

Is Wowayonghtan Navigable all the Way to Ohio

Can Vessels go up the Stream & how Large

Is the Stream rapid —

How far Is it from the Navigable Water of Wou-
bash to Lake Erie

Is Wowbash Navigable all the Way

Is the Stream rapid —

How far from Navigable Water of Siotha to
Creek No 15 that goes into Lake Erie

How from Lower Shawney Town to No 10

How far from No 10 to Missisippi No 2

NATIVE AMERICANS ENCOUNTERED BY LEWIS & CLARK

〜〜〜〜〜

BY THE BEGINNING OF THE NINETEENTH CENTURY,
THE ADMINISTRATION OF PRESIDENT THOMAS JEFFERSON
WAS FACED WITH A DIPLOMATIC CRISIS INVOLVING NEW
ORLEANS AND FRENCH DESIGNS ON SPANISH FLORIDA.

Napoleon Bonaparte, focused on financing a planned war against Great Britain, not only offered to sell New Orleans to the United States, but the entire Louisiana Territory as well. For 15 million dollars (plus 5 million to settle naval claims), the Jefferson administration bought 858,000 square miles of land. Jefferson was interested in having the northwest portion of the North American continent explored even before the purchase, and had secretly charged his private secretary, Meriwether Lewis, with preparing an expedition for that purpose. Lewis asked his former superior, William Clark, an experienced frontiersman, to

share leadership of what would become known as the Corps of Discovery, made up of army men and civilian volunteers. In late 1803, they sailed for St. Louis, made winter camp near the mouth of the Missouri River, and finalized preparations.

Key among Jefferson's objectives for the Corps of Discovery was to establish friendly relations with the dozens of Native American tribes Lewis and Clark would encounter on their journey. Those tribes in the immediate area of the Mississippi, such as the Osage, Quapaw, Fox, and Sauks, were already familiar with Americans as a result of frontier trade conducted along the Mississippi. On May 14, 1804, the 43-man expedition began the ascent of the Missouri River in three boats, two flat-bottom canoes and a keel-boat. The plan was to ascend the Missouri River as far as the Rockies, then portage the craft across the mountains to the Columbia river, which English sea explorers had discovered during their voyages in the northern Pacific.

In July, the expedition began to enter uncharted territory. On the eastern edge of the great prairie lands of present-day Nebraska and Iowa they attempted to make contact with a known tribe, the Pawnee, but they were away on their annual buffalo hunt. Lewis and Clark then encountered previously undiscovered Native Americans, Oto, Missouri, and Arikaras tribesmen. The interpreter in the Corps of Discovery communicated with these Indians in sign language, and despite this inexact method, no major points were lost in

ABOVE Meriwether Lewis and William Clark meet a council of Native Americans from an unspecified tribe in this illustration from an 1810 publication of the journals of the Corps of Discovery.

AMERICAN BISON

When Lewis and Clark came upon the Great Plains west of the Mississippi River, they encountered vast herds of bison. Lacking horses, they themselves did not hunt the animal but the nomadic tribes of the plains, the Cheyenne, Lakota, Shoshone, Yanktonai, Crow, and others, did. Bison provided nearly everything the members of these tribes needed to live. The eastern Siouan cultures had gradually abandoned agriculture when the adoption of the horse gave them greater mobility to chase the bison. Indian and white hunters nearly exhausted the American bison herds by the beginning of the twentieth century and now only a few remain, all of them in captivity or on preserves.

communication. The expedition then encountered the Lakota, the first tribe openly unfriendly to the expedition. The Lakota had a proud tradition as bison hunters and warriors. They demanded tribute from Lewis and Clark for passing across their hunting grounds. A stand-off ensued, but the expedition moved on without a major incident. They made their first winter quarters of the journey at the camp of the Mandan, and also visited the neighboring Hidatsa tribe.

RIGHT Mato-Tope was a chief of the Mandan tribe when he was painted by both George Catlin and Karl Bodmer on their western journeys. He was himself an enthusiastic artist and connected well with the two painters. In this Bodmer watercolor Mato-Tope wears his finest garments and carries a lance decorated with an Arikara scalp. The Arikara warrior killed Mato-Tope's brother and the chief avenged the act by slaying him with this lance.

ABOVE Three Cheyenne warriors overlook the Great Plains in a photograph by Edward Curtis. The Cheyenne along with the Lakota (Teton Sioux) once controlled the Great Plains hunting grounds north of the Arkansas River in what are now western Kansas, Colorado, Wyoming, and southern Montana. But disease, settlement, and military action by the United States government greatly diminished their numbers and power.

ABOVE This illustration shows a buffalo hunt in progress in an area in the shadow of the Rocky Mountains. The bison herds decreased rapidly in the nineteenth century through the combination of Indian and white hunters, and prairie trails and farms that disrupted their migration patterns.

ABOVE This illustration of the interior of a Dakota tipi by P. Rindisbacher shows a group of Indians and a white man, probably a soldier or trader, smoking pipes. Smoking the ceremonial pipe was an element of diplomacy on the plains and could signify peace and agreement. But pipes were also smoked as a prelude to warfare.

Here they copied their notes on the expedition; Lewis was primarily concerned with the scientific discoveries of the trip, Clark with its geographical exploration. In the spring, the keel-boat and a group of the soldiers returned to St. Louis with journals and samples of the expedition's discoveries to date. Lewis and Clark hired a French Canadian to join the expedition, Toussaint Charbonneau, who brought his Shoshonean bride, Sacajawea, and their infant son with him. Lewis and Clark were reluctant to have a woman and papoose on the rugged journey, but Sacajawea's aid proved to be invaluable to the expedition.

In late spring, they encountered the foothills of the Rockies, began the ascent on foot, and then came to a Shoshonean village. Obtaining horses, they crossed the mountains, and in October met the friendly Nez Percé, who told of a water passage westward. Building new smaller canoes, the party navigated the western Rockies via the Clearwater and Snake rivers and arrived at the mouth of the Columbia River before the onset of winter. They built a fort on the Pacific Coast but failed to make much progress in striking trade negotiations with the coastal tribes, who had been trading with European sailing expeditions for decades. With the coming of spring, the

SACAJAWEA

Sacajawea, a Shoshone, was captured as a teenager by a Hidatsa war party and sold to French Canadian trapper Toussaint Charbonneau, who married her. In the spring of 1805, when Charbonneau was hired by Lewis and Clark for their expedition to the Rocky Mountains and beyond, Sacajawea and their infant son went along. She proved to be an invaluable guide for the expedition. When they reached a Shoshone village, she was reunited with her brother, Cameahwait, the village chief. Sacajawea acted as an interpreter for Lewis and Clark and helped them obtain horses from her brother's tribe. She accompanied the expedition to the Pacific Ocean and on the return east to a Mandan village, where she and her family bade goodbye to the great explorers.

expedition, having failed to make contact with any American vessel on the Pacific coast, returned over the mountains, exploring different routes part of the way, and returned to a heroes' welcome in St. Louis. Although the Corps of Discovery achieved their goals of exploration and negotiating peaceful trade pacts, they also unwittingly opened the door for the massive western settlement that would forever change the Native American cultures of the Great Plains and beyond.

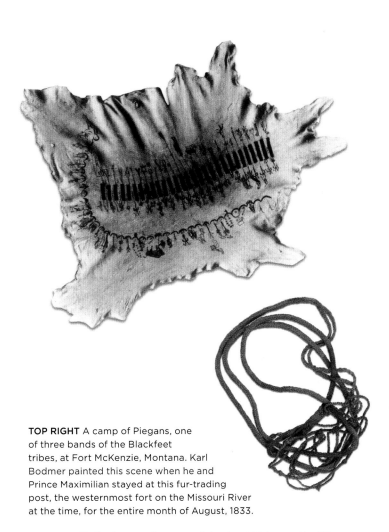

TOP RIGHT A camp of Piegans, one of three bands of the Blackfeet tribes, at Fort McKenzie, Montana. Karl Bodmer painted this scene when he and Prince Maximilian stayed at this fur-trading post, the westernmost fort on the Missouri River at the time, for the entire month of August, 1833.

ABOVE LEFT The Kiowa tribe roamed the Great Plains south of the Missouri River, the principal water route of the Corps of Discovery. Many Plains Indian tribes used the technique displayed in this Kiowa calendar—recording the passage of time by illustrating notable events on a cured animal hide.

ABOVE RIGHT This animal snare, made of yucca fiber, was found in a cave in McElmo Canyon in southwestern Colorado. Snares were used by hunters across the Great Plains and Rockies to capture small game.

ABOVE In 1833 Bodmer created this watercolor of a Mandan looking up at a sacred shrine. The two poles represented the Creator and the Woman Who Never Dies, the former a shrine to the Giver of Life, and the latter the eternal provider of subsistence to the tribe. The shrine protected a Mandan village's burial site.

INDIAN BUREAUS &
THE FIRST RESERVATIONS

WHEN THOMAS JEFFERSON PROCLAIMED THE INDIANS
WERE EQUALS TO THE WHITE MAN IN EVERY WAY,
HE SECRETLY HOPED THIS EQUALITY WOULD BE PRACTICED
MAINLY IN THE LANDS WEST OF THE MISSISSIPPI RIVER.

Like many of his contemporaries, he did not suppose that the incorporation of Native Americans into the burgeoning white settlements of the east would be a smooth transition. Though the British treaty on Indian sovereignty was struck down by the United States Supreme Court under Chief Justice John Marshall, the decision would not be Marshall's final word on the subject.

The American president who was most fervent in pushing for a policy of Indian "removal" (as it was then termed) was Andrew Jackson. His interest in white expansion was demonstrated by his actions in Florida beginning in 1817. In sharing Jefferson's secret views, Jackson was far more vocal on the subject. Indian Affairs received bureau-level status in the executive branch before Jackson's presidency, however he was the first to use the spreading influence of Indian agents to secure pacts which drove Native Americans from their homelands.

While some of the eastern tribes, already virtually decimated by disease and conflict, gave in to the establishment of the reservation system, those in the Old

LEFT Karl Bodmer, one of the European artists who traveled throughout the United States in the first part of the nineteenth century painting Native Americans with his employer and expedition chronicler, Prince Maximilian, painted the detailed watercolor in this lithograph. The subjects are from left, a Missouri Indian, an Oto Indian, and a chief of the Poncas, who is wearing a large American peace medal. Bodmer painted on-site and whether or not he got these three individuals to pose together, they were probably painted in 1833 as Maximilian and Bodmer traveled the Missouri River on the riverboat *Yellowstone*.

OSCEOLA

Osceola was the son of a Creek woman, a member of the "Red Sticks" portion of the Creek nation who fled to Florida after the defeat at Horseshoe Bend. He grew to the status of an elite warrior among the fugitives and gained the trust and respect of the Seminoles who had long established a home in Florida. When he became chief he incurred the wrath of Andrew Jackson by accepting runaway slaves into the tribe's fold. Jackson used the tenets of the Runaway Slave laws as legal justification to wage war on the Seminoles after Osceola rejected a removal treaty that offered the tribe only two cents an acre for their land. Osceola and his warriors—including some African Americans—eluded United States troops for two years until he was captured in the fall of 1837. Osceola died in captivity at Fort Moultrie, South Carolina, in 1838, but the Seminoles carried on the fight until defeated in this, the Second Seminole War, in 1842.

FAR LEFT A bison at rest on the Great Plains. Though many thousands of animals roamed the prairie at the beginning of the nineteenth century, the number dwindled to hundreds by the end of the century. At that time a new processing technique created a demand for their hide as a leather source, so white "hide men" killed thousands. This action also deterred free-roaming plains tribes from hunting bison off the reservation and greatly contributed to pushing the animal toward extinction.

LEFT Abraham Quary was listed as the last of the Nantucket tribe in this lithograph of an 1834 sketch by Jerome Thompson. He posed for Thompson on Nantucket Island when he was a 64-year-old chief.

BELOW LEFT Fort Laramie, pictured here in a late-nineteenth-century photograph, began as a trading post on the Oregon Trail and in 1849 was converted to an army outpost. Here in 1851 a landmark peace treaty was arranged by Indian Agent Thomas Fitzpatrick and signed by chiefs of eight major northern plains tribes. It provided for the peaceful passage of settlers and traders and divided hunting grounds along tribal lines.

LEFT *The Last of the Shinnecock Indians* is the title of this photograph taken on Long Island in 1889. Whether or not they were the last is unsure, but like other eastern tribes many members were wiped out by disease, married non-Native Americans, or were assimilated into the Euro-American culture. The Shinnecock maintain a small reservation on eastern Long Island.

Northwest did not. After the Indians of Ohio, Indiana, Michigan, and Illinois lost their homelands by, among other reasons, backing the British in the War of 1812, they were driven to the west side of the Mississippi, or to the area of the river's source in what are now the states of Wisconsin and Minnesota.

In the south, the situation was different. Those tribes that suffered most in squabbles between themselves and with the white man, such as the Tutelo, Catawba, and Pamunkey, found their surviving members reduced to living on reservations that represented a tiny portion of the lands they had once controlled. However, further south resistance to removal was more prevalent. Particularly well organized in their objections were the Cherokee, whose territory once covered much of western North Carolina, Tennessee, northeast Alabama, and northwest Georgia. In 1795, they signed a treaty that greatly reduced their holdings and confined the Cherokee Nation to an area encompassing northwest Georgia and small parts of Tennessee and Alabama. The capital of their well-educated and, for the most part, prosperous population was New Echota. They continued to refine their culture and shape their national republic after the model of the United States.

By the time Andrew Jackson came to power in 1829, the landscape had changed, literally. Not only were white settlers taking over Cherokee lands, with a small find of gold complicating matters, but the State of Georgia had passed laws making it almost impossible for the Cherokee to maintain control of their land. The tribe challenged the law in the federal court system and this time Justice Marshall used a case

involving two U.S. citizens arrested for helping the Cherokee, to rule (in February 1832) in favor of the Indians and strike down the Georgia law. But Jackson made it clear he would not use federal government resources to enforce the decision. Land violations continued unabated and, more seriously, the Cherokee council split into two factions: those resigned to removal to a new federal Indian Territory north of the Red River, and those who insisted on standing their ground.

The first of the Cherokee left Georgia in 1835, while others held out until 1838 when federal troops were called in to enforce the removal, made official by the Indian Removal Act of 1830 that established the Indian Territory. Those that held out to the end not only lost many of their possessions, they also suffered privations when they were rounded up and held in temporary stockades before being boarded on steamers for their new homes. Once there, they were not only forced to compete for prime land with those Cherokees who had left Georgia earlier, but also with three other relocated tribes, the Choctaw, Chickasaw, and Creeks. The Cherokees called the difficult and deadly journey the "Trail of Tears." The last of the Five Civilized Tribes—as they were known in the mid-nineteenth century—to arrive in Indian Territory were the Seminoles, who fought the United States in military actions initiated by Jackson and termed the Second and Third Seminole Wars (1835–42 and 1855–58). Under their leaders Osceola, and others, the Seminoles of Florida were the last of the major tribes east of the Mississippi to be forced onto reservations or out of their homelands entirely.

INDIAN AGENTS

In 1789 the federal government established an arm of the War Department to deal with the Indians, but in 1824 Secretary of War John C. Calhoun reorganized the Indian Department into a separate entity, the Bureau of Indian Affairs (B.I.A.). By that time, Indian agents, such as Albert Pike shown here, were already in the field, negotiating the deals and treaties that forced tribes to move onto reservations. The agents then issued the monetary awards, annual stipends, and supplies to the tribes, operating from established offices or agencies. While some individual agents crusaded for fair treatment, most simply carried out the insensitive policies established in Washington to herd Indians onto increasingly smaller tracts of land.

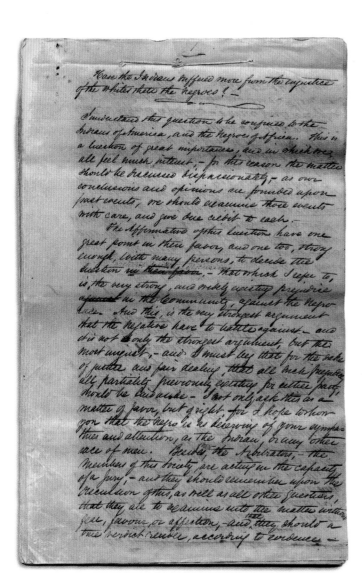

ABOVE Seven mounted Spokane men look over a tributary of their namesake river in this Edward Curtis photograph. The tribe was later confined to the small Spokane Reservation in northeast Washington.

LEFT On January 9, 1849, New York attorney H. W. Eastman gave a lecture in which he compared the treatment of Native Americans and African Americans by Euro-Americans. He presented a large amount of evidence to support his argument that Indians suffered from their own "indolence" rather than white injustice, while African slaves were clearly mistreated by whites. Eastman's arguments were pro-abolition yet also for assimilating or "civilizing" the Native Americans at a time when both topics were emotionally debated.

RIGHT An Indian burial ground, of unknown tribal affiliation.

Touch-the-Cloud School,

CHEYENNE RIVER, SO. DAK.

MISSIONARY STATION, No. 7.

DAKOTA.	WAŚICUN.	DAKOTA.	WAŚICUN.
1 Numkte.	Killed by two.	21 Cablewin.	Slicer.
2 Wapaha.	Hat.	22 Tasagyewin	Staff.
3 Otaagli.	Brings many.	23 Śunkawakanwin.	Horse.
4 Tunweyaagli.	Returns from scouting.	24 Tokaicuwawin	Pursues the enemy with.
5 Kaĥniń kte.	Kills his choice.	25 Hantela.	Little Cedar.
6 Pejuta.	Medicine.	26 Glokuwin.	Brings home.
7 Kipajinpi.	Accused.	27 Inihanwin.	Scared.
8 Glihpeyela.	Falls at home.	28 Wahacankataninkiyewin.	Raises the spear.
9 Śunkahiyanjica.	Dog down.	29 Ptesanwanmli.	Eagle white cow.
10 Okisewakan.	Half holy.	30 Ptesanwaśtewin.	Good white cow.
11 Hanhepi kte.	Killed at night.	31 Taśinatokecawin.	Strange robe.
12 Wanikiskan.	Becomes active.	32 Heunhawin.	Buries with the horn.
13 Bliheiçiya.	Industrious.	33 Hemaza.	Iron horn.
14 Stilikte.	Pawnee killer.	34 Ptesanwin.	White cow.
15 Wicagloku.	Brings them home.	35 Taĥcainipiwin.	Deer sweat bath.
16 Kawociṅśica.	Makes cross.	36 Tasagyewin.	Staff.
17 Paĥpapi.	Cast down.	37 Taĥcaiçiblecawin.	Deer that shakes itself.
18 Hinhanhotewin.	Gray owl.	38 Pinzaktewin.	Prairie dog killer.
19 Śunkagleśkawin.	Spotted horse.	39 Howaśtewin.	Pretty voice.
20 Hepinkpawin.	Horn's end.	40 Kiciyankela.	Staying with.

DAKOTA WORD LIST

This word list in Dakota and Wasicun was used by missionaries at the Touch-the-Cloud School on the Cheyenne River in South Dakota. It translated common phrases into English. *Wasicun* was a word used by Plains tribes referring to whites.

ORDERS. No. 25.

Head Quarters, Eastern Division. Cherokee Agency, Ten. May 17, 1838.

MAJOR GENERAL SCOTT, of the United States' Army, announces to the troops assembled and assembling in this country, that, with them, he has been charged by the President to cause the Cherokee Indians yet remaining in North Carolina, Georgia, Tennessee and Alabama, to remove to the West, according to the terms of the Treaty of 1835. His Staff will be as follows:

LIEUTENANT COLONEL W. J. WORTH, acting Adjutant General, Chief of the Staff.

MAJOR M. M. PAYNE, acting Inspector General.

LIEUTENANTS R. ANDERSON, & E. D. KEYES, regular Aids-de-camp.

COLONEL A. H. KENAN & LIEUTENANT H. B. SHAW, volunteer Aids-de-camp.

Any order given orally, or in writing, by either of those officers, in the name of the Major General, will be respected and obeyed as if given by himself.

The Chiefs of Ordnance, of the Quarter-Master's Department and of the Commissariat, as also the Medical Director of this Army, will, as soon as they can be ascertained, be announced in orders.

To carry out the general object with the greatest promptitude and certainty, and with the least possible distress to the Indians, the country they are to evacuate will be divided into three principal Military Districts, under as many officers of high rank, to command the troops serving therein, subject to the instructions of the Major General.

Eastern District, to be commanded by BRIGADIER GENERAL EUSTIS, of the United States' Army, or the highest officer in rank, serving therein:—North Carolina, the part of Tennessee lying north of Gilmer county, Georgia, and the counties of Gilmer, Union, and Lumpkin, in Georgia. Head Quarters, in the first instance, say, at Fort Butler.

Western District, to be commanded by COLONEL LINDSAY, of the United States' Army, or the highest officer in rank serving therein:—Alabama, the residue of Tennessee and Dade county, in Georgia. Head quarters, in the first instance, say, at Ross' Landing.

Middle District, to be commanded by BRIGADIER GENERAL ARMISTEAD of the United States' Army, or the highest officer in rank, serving therein:—All that part of the Cherokee country, lying within the State of Georgia, and which is not comprised in the two other districts. Head Quarters, in the first instance, say, at New Echota.

It is not intended that the foregoing boundaries between the principal commanders shall be strictly observed. Either, when carried near the district of another, will not hesitate to extend his operations, according to the necessities of the case, but with all practicable harmony, into the adjoining district. And, among his principal objects, in case of actual or apprehended hostilities, will be that of affording adequate protection to our white people in and around the Cherokee country.

The senior officer actually present in each district will receive instructions from the Major General as to the time of commencing the removal, and every thing that may occur interesting to the service, in the district, will be promptly reported to the same source. The Major General will endeavour to visit in a short time all parts of the Cherokee country occupied by the troops.

The duties devolved on the army, through the orders of the Major General & those of the commanders of districts, under him, are of a highly important and critical nature.

The Cherokees, by the advances which they have made in christianity and civilization, are by far the most interesting tribe of Indians in the territorial limits of the United States. Of the 15,000 of those people who are now to be removed—(and the time within which a voluntary emigration was stipulated, will expire on the 23rd instant—) it is understood that about four fifths are opposed, or have become averse to a distant emigration; and altho' none are in actual hostilities with the United States, or threaten a resistance by arms, yet the troops will probably be obliged to cover the whole country they inhabit, in order to make prisoners and to march or to transport the prisoners, by families, either to this place, to Ross' Landing or Gunter's Landing, where they are to be finally delivered over to the Superintendant of Cherokee Emigration.

Considering the number and temper of the mass to be removed, together with the extent and fastnesses of the country occupied, it will readily occur, that simple indiscretions—acts of harshness and cruelty, on the part of our troops, may lead, step by step, to delays, to impatience and exasperation, and in the end, to a general war and carnage—a result, in the case of those particular Indians, utterly abhorrent to the generous sympathies of the whole American people. Every possible kindness, compatible with the necessity of removal, must, therefore, be shown by the troops, and, if, in the ranks, a despicable individual should be found, capable of inflicting a wanton injury or insult on any Cherokee man, woman or child, it is hereby made the special duty of the nearest good officer or man, instantly to interpose, and to seize and consign the guilty wretch to the severest penalty of the laws. The Major General is fully persuaded that this injunction will not be neglected by the brave men under his command, who cannot be otherwise than jealous of their own honor and that of their country.

By early and persevering acts of kindness and humanity, it is impossible to doubt that the Indians may soon be induced to confide in the Army, and instead of fleeing to mountains and forests, flock to us for food and clothing. If, however, through false apprehensions, individuals, or a party, here and there, should seek to hide themselves, they must be pursued and invited to surrender, but not fired upon unless they should make a stand to resist. Even in such cases, mild remedies may sometimes better succeed than violence; and it cannot be doubted that if we get possession of the women and children first, or first capture the men, that, in either case, the outstanding members of the same families will readily come in on the assurance of forgiveness and kind treatment.

Every captured man, as well as all who surrender themselves, must be disarmed, with the assurance that their weapons will be carefully preserved and restored at, or beyond the Mississippi. In either case, the men will be guarded and escorted, except it may be, where their women and children are safely secured as hostages; but, in general, families, in our possession, will not be separated, unless it be to send men, as runners, to invite others to come in.

It may happen that Indians will be found too sick, in the opinion of the nearest Surgeon, to be removed to one of the depots indicated above. In every such case, one or more of the family, or the friends of the sick person, will be left in attendance, with ample subsistence and remedies, and the remainder of the family removed by the troops. Infants, superannuated persons, lunatics and women in a helpless condition, will all, in the removal, require peculiar attention, which the brave and humane will seek to adapt to the necessities of the several cases.

All strong men, women, boys & girls, will be made to march under proper escorts. For the feeble, Indian horses and ponies will furnish a ready resource, as well as for bedding and light cooking utensils—all of which, as intimated in the Treaty, will be necessary to the emigrants both in going to, and after arrival at, their new homes. Such, and all other light articles of property, the Indians will be allowed to collect and to take with them, as also their slaves, who will be treated in like manner with the Indians themselves.

If the horses and ponies be not adequate to the above purposes, wagons must be supplied.

Corn, oats, fodder and other forage, also beef cattle, belonging to the Indians to be removed, will be taken possession of by the proper departments of the Staff, as wanted, for the regular consumption of the Army, and certificates given to the owners, specifying in every case, the amount of forage and the weight of beef, so taken, in order that the owners may be paid for the same on their arrival at one of the depots mentioned above.

All other moveable or personal property, left or abandoned by the Indians, will be collected by agents appointed for the purpose, by the Superintendant of Cherokee Emigration, under a system of accountability, for the benefit of the Indian owners, which he will devise. The Army will give to those agents, in their operations, all reasonable countenance, aid and support.

White men and widows, citizens of the United States, who are, or have been intermarried with Indians, and thence commonly termed, *Indian countrymen*; also such Indians as have been made denizens of particular States by special legislation, together with the families and property of all such persons, will not be molested or removed by the troops until a decision, on the principles involved, can be obtained from the War Department.

A like indulgence, but only for a limited time, and until further orders, is extended to the families and property of certain Chiefs and head-men of the two great Indian parties, (on the subject of emigration) now understood to be absent in the direction of Washington on the business of their respective parties.

This order will be carefully read at the head of every company in the Army.

By Command:

W. L. WORTH, Lt. Col.
Chief of the Staff

Winfield Scott

GOLD & SETTLERS CHALLENGE CALIFORNIA TRIBES

LIKE THEIR NEIGHBORS TO THE SOUTH, THE NATIVE AMERICAN TRIBES OF NORTHERN AND INLAND CENTRAL CALIFORNIA, AS WELL AS THOSE DESERT TRADITION TRIBES BETWEEN THE SIERRA NEVADA AND ROCKY MOUNTAINS, SELDOM RESORTED TO VIOLENCE OR INTERTRIBAL WARFARE TO SETTLE DISPUTES.

ABOVE Winnemucca, the Paiute Chief of western Nevada and father of Sarah Winnemucca, poses for a photographer in 1880. Winnemucca was the son-in-law and successor of Paiute chief Jack Truckee, a friend of whites who fought the Spanish in California alongside John C. Frémont. Winnemucca tried to maintain tribal lands and keep the peace, but anxious warriors under Numaga battled settlers at Pyramid Lake in 1860. Violence, mining, and settlers forced the tribe from Pyramid Lake into an inhospitable desert.

This was primarily because there were fewer members of each tribe and the sparseness of the populations made the kind of political organization and tribal rivalry issues that bring on warfare untenable. The tribes were also skilled basketmakers, engaged in elaborate coming-of-age rituals and did not participate in any kind of agriculture.

There were, however, sharp differences between those tribes living on or near the coast and those east of the Sierra Nevada, especially in the means of acquiring food. It was only the coming of the white man that would give these groups a common cause. Those on the coastal plain, the Hupa, Pomo, Yuki tribes, and others, enjoyed abundant opportunities for gathering wild plant foods and fishing. Rivers flowed freely in Northern California and fish were speared or netted there to supplement the gathering of mollusks and other sea creatures. Even sea mammals, such as the sea lion and otter, were trapped and used for food and clothing. Some tribes hunted in the mountain foothills.

For those tribes to the east, the Mono, Washo, Paiute, and others, the arid conditions which prevailed for most of the year made food gathering more difficult. The rivers and streams fed by the eastern Sierra Nevada snowcap and other ranges allowed some fishing. A large variety of mammals were hunted. For those to the east, however, the desert conditions forced the women to seek out edible seeds and roots, and harvest insects;

SARAH WINNEMUCCA

Sarah was the daughter of a Northern Paiute chief, and was educated at a California women's college. She became an interpreter and scout and married a U.S. Army officer. In 1878, the Bannocks of Idaho waged a short war with the army, and the Northern Paiutes were considering joining their ranks. Sarah foresaw the destructive effect a war with the well-organized U.S. Army force would bring, and traveled between the lines to convince her father and his warriors not to go into battle. She was abandoned by her first officer husband but married another officer and later in life founded a school for Indian children.

BELOW LEFT Residents of the Round Valley Reservation pose in front of the Agency Office and Sutler Store in 1876. The northern California federal farm was one of seven established shortly after California became a state to force Indians off their ancestral lands for gold mining and other forms of white economic exploitation. The reservation brought together Yokuts, Pomos, and members of other tribes who were unaccustomed to living together.

BELOW RIGHT Edward Curtis called this misty scene Smokey Day at the Sugar Bowl. The northern California Hupa man is fishing with a wooden spear, a common method of catching salmon and other stream fish in the Trinity River Hupa homeland.

while the men went after the small mammals and reptiles that made the desert home, particularly the jackrabbit. All desert creatures were hunted except the coyote, an animal considered sacred by the Paiute and other tribes of the desert.

As with the Mission Indians, the coming of the white man changed lifestyles which had endured for several millennia. Except for a few tribes impacted by the northern string of missions and seaside ports along the coast, the storm clouds would come from the east, in the form of settlers and, from 1849, gold and silver prospectors and those that followed in their wake.

ABOVE These Indian scouts pictured at the lava beds in central California were part of a military force sent in pursuit of Captain Jack and his Modoc band in 1873. Eadweard Muybridge, creator of this photograph, was a pioneer in using the camera for the study of human anatomy.

ABOVE This 1874 photograph shows a Uintah Ute in full war dress and a youth carrying a large decorated shoulder bag on their traditional mounts, ponies. By the late 1800s the Uintah were forced onto a desolate reservation in eastern Utah. After a short war in 1879 their close kin, the White River Utes of western Colorado, were forced onto the reservation as well.

In 1848, while constructing a sawmill on the American River, John Marshall, a foreman on a tract of land owned by John Sutter, discovered gold flakes in the water while the mill race was being constructed. After a trip to the provincial capital of Monterey to authenticate and file the claim, Sutter quickly changed the purpose of his property to mining. He had built a fort to protect his property near present-day Sacramento, but that was not enough to keep his land and Indian land free from hundreds of gold-seekers, squatting along the rivers and tributaries to pan gold from the silt-laden waters. Finds of gold, and particularly silver, in underground veins led prospectors to Nevada as well. Finally, the pilgrimage of another persecuted people, the Mormons, led to the establishment of a large colony in Utah from 1847, completing the incursion of whites into the lands of the Desert Tradition.

The impact on the Indians was immediate and tragic. Many were pressed into the service of the prospectors as indentured servants. Others found their prime fishing areas and gathering spots spoiled by the damming streams and the rapid building of boomtowns. The Indians here lacked the warrior tradition of the neighboring plains tribes, and were poorly prepared to fight for their homelands. The United States government quickly made the area, won in a decisive victory over Mexico in 1848, into the states of California in 1850, then Nevada in 1864. The Indians could only stand aside and watch with sadness the devastating effects of the "Gold Rush". One of the exceptions, however, was an 1862 attack on settlers in California's Owens Valley, east of the Sierra Nevada, in which United States troops were called out to put down the uprising.

POMO BASKETRY ARTISTS

Many Native American cultures made and used baskets (a general classification for containers constructed of grass or plant fiber), but the women of the Pomo tribe on the central Californian coast have been judged the finest by archeologists and anthropologists who have studied their work. They used both twining and coiling techniques with geometric patterns in a soothing rhythm. The containers were made in many different designs, with unusually shaped examples used for rituals. The baskets were often decorated with the colorful shells of abalone to give them a truly unique appearance.

ABOVE This Hupa female shaman wears a headband and dentalium necklace and holds two small baskets in a photograph by Edward Curtis, part of his study of Athapascan cultures of the northwest. Dentalium was a prized shell to the Hupa, considered a reward from the Immortals, and used as currency and in important ceremonies such as the "World Renewal" ceremonies.

LEFT This hunting basket was passed between the Yokuts, who lived west of the Sierra Mountains in California's central valley and foothills, and the Mono Band, who lived east of the range. It signaled the beginning of the hunting season in which the two tribes cooperated.

NATIVE AMERICANS & THE CIVIL WAR

THE ROLE OF NATIVE AMERICANS IN THE CIVIL WAR IS MORE THAN JUST A HISTORICAL FOOTNOTE. ORGANIZED GROUPS OF WARRIORS, ALLIED TO EITHER THE UNION OR CONFEDERACY, TOOK PART IN BATTLES, JOINED THE FORCES OF THE NORTH OR SOUTH INDIVIDUALLY, ACTED AS SCOUTS, OR FORMED INDIAN HOME GUARD UNITS.

The Five Civilized Tribes of the Indian Territory, feeling antipathy toward the government that removed them from their land, and with economic and cultural ties to the states of the South, contributed the greatest support for the Confederacy among Native American tribes. The first large-scale test of Native American fighters came as warriors of these tribes joined Texas volunteers to oppose a federal force at Pea Ridge, Arkansas, on March 7–8, 1862.

LEFT The Battle of Pea Ridge, fought March 7–8, 1862, was the first major Civil War engagement in which Native American forces fought for the South. Mounted Cherokees made up a portion of Major General Earl Van Dorn's command, but the well-positioned Federal forces with their line of artillery quickly scattered the Indians and drove them from the field on March 8. This fanciful period lithograph incorrectly portrayed the Cherokee fighters in war bonnets.

ABOVE Though reluctant at first, Chief Little Crow led the Dakota on raids against white settlers in the Minnesota River Valley and then clashed with soldiers until defeated at Wood Lake. He fled to Dakota but returned to Minnesota with a few companions in 1863 and was killed by two farmers.

ABOVE Fort Snelling, Minnesota, at the confluence of the Mississippi and Minnesota Rivers, was a strategic trading center and military outpost before the Civil War. During the war it served as regional headquarters for Major General John Pope and other U.S. Army officials, and as a prison camp for captured warriors.

ABOVE The Santee Sioux (Dakota) under Little Crow terrorized settlements in western Minnesota during the 1862 uprising. Here a group of frightened women and children, led by armed men, pause to rest in their flight from the area.

A number of Indian revolts took place during the Civil War. The Dakota—then known as the Santee Sioux, and Minnesota's main tribe—had sold most of their land to the federal government in 1851, and were moved to a reservation along the Minnesota River. But as the Civil War progressed, white immigration into the state continued to increase. In August 1862, under Chief Little Crow, they attacked settlers in the vicinity of the Lower Sioux Agency, killing 800 during the uprising, taking prisoners, destroying property, and driving the survivors into Fort Ridgely. On August 18, they attacked the agency and assaulted Fort Ridgely on August 20 and 22, but the

garrison there held. The Sioux attacked the German settlement of New Ulm on August 19 and 25, but were driven off by the settlers there. On September 2, at Birch Coulee, Sioux warriors surprised a camp of Minnesota volunteers and pinned them down for 36 hours until relief arrived.

Alarmed at these developments, the Governor of Minnesota commissioned Henry Hastings Sibley as colonel and put him in charge of newly-enlisted Minnesota volunteers. On September 19, Sibley's expedition of 1,400 set out from Fort Ridgely to put down the uprising. On September 23, at Wood Lake, near the Upper Sioux Agency, the Minnesota soldiers dealt Little Crow

ELY PARKER

Ely S. Parker was an educated Seneca who was practicing law in Galena, Illinois, at the outbreak of the Civil War. There he met Ulysses S. Grant. When Grant became commander of the Division of Southern Illinois and Eastern Missouri, he invited Parker to join his headquarters staff. Parker rose to the rank of colonel and wrote out the terms of the Confederate surrender at Appomattox. When Grant became president in 1869, he appointed Parker Commissioner of Indian Affairs, the first Native American in the post. But Parker was a victim of the political corruption scandals that wracked the Grant administration and he was forced to resign the post. He died in poverty in 1895.

LEFT President Abraham Lincoln is shown receiving Comanche leaders at the Executive Mansion, as the White House was called then, in this period hand-colored etching. Though Lincoln spent most of his presidency focused on winning the Civil War, he still had many other duties, including working for a reduction of friction between Native Americans and settlers in the Great Plains region.

a serious defeat, capturing 2,000 and scattering the rest. Little Crow fled with a number of his followers to Dakota Territory. In total 307 captured warriors were tried and found responsible for the uprising. President Abraham Lincoln pardoned all but 38 who were hanged in Mankato on December 26, 1862, in the largest public execution in U.S. history.

In the summer of 1863, as the Dakota Territory was being settled, Major General John Pope launched a two-pronged offensive against the Dakota before they could harass homesteaders. In July, Sibley led a force against the Dakota, who had joined forces with their Nakota and Lakota brethren. On July 24, Sibley advanced on a "big mound" rising from among the ravines, and with artillery support scattered the warriors. After the Battle of Big Mound, Sibley pursued the Dakota and broke the force in two more actions, at Dead Buffalo Lake on July 26 and Stone Lake on July 28.

The other prong of Pope's offensive was a force under Brigadier General Alfred Sully. On September 3, 1863, at Whitestone Hill, Sully's men routed the Indians from their camp. Sully's force of 2,500 then advanced and established Fort Rice at the mouth of the Cannonball River on July 7, 1864. Pope sent infantry to back up Sully and the army built more forts. The cavalry continued west and found a large camp on the Little Missouri River. After a conference with tribal leaders

failed, Sully attacked the camp at Killdeer Mountain on July 28 and the warriors gave ground. The Battle of Killdeer Mountain broke the back of the Sioux resistance and allowed a new military presence that kept the area relatively peaceful until the end of the Civil War.

Indian Territory saw battles between the North and South during the middle years of the war. Former Indian agents who gained general commissions encouraged Cherokees and others to join the Confederacy. But Native Americans loyal to the Union formed units in Kansas and Missouri under white officers, and marched south to oppose these Rebels. At Chustenahlah (1861), Old Fort Wayne (1862), and Honey Springs (1863), as well as other places in Indian Territory and the Trans-Mississippi region, the Confederates scored a few victories, but ultimately the Rebel forces were contained, then destroyed by the Federals.

The Chiricahua Apache role in the war against the United States began in 1861 when a well-known chief, Cochise, was falsely accused of a raid and the incident led to bloodshed. Then in a skirmish at Apache Pass, Arizona, he escaped U.S. soldiers under Lieutenant George Bascom. From that point, Cochise and his band harassed the whites in the area including Brigadier General Carlton's California column, which was marching from Tucson to New Mexico to aid in the fight against Confederate soldiers there. After several patrols were ambushed, Carlton sent a force that on July 15–16, 1862, managed to dislodge the Apaches under Cochise and Mangas Colorado. Carlton then ordered a detachment to build Fort Bowie at Apache Pass.

In another sad chapter in American history, Colonel John Chivington, who had a successful Civil War record previously, inflicted a major injustice on peaceful Native Americans in Colorado. Backed by the governor of that state, Chivington massacred several hundred Cheyenne and Arapaho under Chief Black Kettle at Sand Creek, Colorado in November 1864. Another unjustified massacre of Native Americans had occurred at Bear Creek in Idaho the previous year.

In November 1864, General Carlton formed an expedition of more than 800 soldiers and Indian allies under Christopher "Kit" Carson to move against warriors attacking whites on the Santa Fe Trail. After a few weeks on the march in the Texas panhandle the force came upon a village of about 1,000 Kiowa which Carson attacked at dawn on November 25. But as the soldiers continued their advance toward an old trading post known as Adobe Walls, they were met by a number of Kiowa and Comanche braves that equaled their own. Carson was able to extricate his force under artillery fire and on the withdrawal back to New Mexico he destroyed the Kiowa village.

FAR LEFT Chief Black Kettle was the most conciliatory to whites of all Cheyenne leaders in the mid-nineteenth century. He even led a peace delegation through the streets of Denver in 1864. The answer he received from the over-zealous governor of Colorado was the destruction of his village at Sand Creek. Though Black Kettle continued to work for peace, he could not control Cheyenne "Dog Soldiers" and he was finally killed by troopers from the U.S. 7th Cavalry in the 1868 Battle of Washita.

LEFT Douglas Cooper was a U.S. Indian agent who gained the trust of Cherokees and others who sympathized with the rebellious South in the Civil War. He was appointed commander of the Confederate Indian Department and was later promoted from colonel to brigadier general. Cooper battled against Chief Opothleyahola and his Creeks and Seminoles in 1861–62 but his army was dealt its serious blow by a superior Union force in the Battle of Honey Springs on July 17, 1863.

STAND WATIE

Stand Watie was a Cherokee living in Indian Territory at the outbreak of the Civil War. He was a close relative of the highly educated group of Cherokees who formed the delegation that opposed the Indian Removal Act of 1830 in U.S. Courts. A wealthy planter, Watie formed a command drawn from the Five Civilized Tribes exiled to the territory: the Cherokee, Choctaw, Chickasaw, Creek, and Seminole. A clever tactician, he never experienced a defeat at the hands of the Federal Army. After the war, he saw his land holdings in the territory reduced as punishment for taking up arms against the federal government.

PEACE LETTER

With the help of a sympathetic U.S. Indian agent, Chief Black Kettle composed this "peace letter" and personally delivered it to the Colorado Territorial Governor, Joseph Brown, in Denver. It did not quell the governor's ambition to rid the territory of Native Americans to attract more white settlement. Black Kettle vainly waved the document in the air during the Sand Creek Massacre.

Names of Indian prisoners pardoned

Tapeta Tanka   Maza adidi
Tahohpi wakan   Tate Ibomdu
Wakanhdito
Tate sica
Wirjuha
Tunkan Oyateyanka
Pantaninmiye
Conkdoka duta
Kinyan hiyaya
Wiyaka
Kinyan hidan
Oye Maza
Cinkpa tawa
Tunkan Canhdeska
Wakaninapedan or Maza Kiyemani
Katpantpan ku
Tahokage
Tunkan hnamani
Boyaya
Iyasa mani
Teaduze
Manikiya
Ahotonna

Pardoned to day, April 30, 1864

32712

LINCOLN'S PARDON

This document, in President Lincoln's own hand, lists the names of 25 Dakota warriors who were held in custody after the Sioux uprising of 1862, but were given presidential pardon in 1864. They and others escaped the mass hanging at Mankato in December 1862.

FARMERS, RANCHERS & NATIVE AMERICANS

BY THE 1860S, THE UNITED STATES HAD COMPLETED THE ACQUISITION,
BY TREATY, PURCHASE OR CONQUEST, OF THE TERRITORY THAT
WOULD EVENTUALLY MAKE UP THE 48 CONTIGUOUS STATES.

The end of the Civil War in 1865 had reunited the country and the dream of Manifest Destiny—the building of a continuous nation from Atlantic to Pacific—was once again achievable. But that was for the white nation. What about the Indian nation? For the Native Americans, it was a land of shrinking territory and resources. Those tribes that had been pushed west of the Mississippi River now found that white settlers were competing with them for the resources on which they depended. Their hold on viable hunting and farming land was reduced to just those areas where reservations were created or land set aside for them by an ever changing inventory of treaties.

The Indians of the Great Plains considered the vast area between the Mississippi and Rocky Mountains as their open hunting ground and they challenged the white settlements in new ways. They tolerated the initial incursions of the whites

ABOVE After the Civil War this group of Cherokee leaders went to Washington to appeal the case of their people in the face of the planned U.S. policy to carve other reservations out of their land to punish those Cherokees who fought for the Confederacy. Among those pictured are John Rollins Ridge, son of John Ridge (left), Saladin Watie, son of Stand Watie (second from left), and Elias Cornelius Boudinot, son of Elias Boudinot (second from right).

ABOVE A sketch of Native American gumbo sellers at New Orleans French Market. Members of the Opelousas, Coushatta, Chitimacha, Bayougoula, and other tribes eluded efforts by the expanding white population to push them onto reservations and faded into the bayous. They would bring food products from their catches and harvests to the city to sell and support themselves.

CEREMONIAL DANCES OF THE PLAINS TRIBES

Plains Indians held many kinds of rituals. Sun dances are among the most famous. This is a generic term for a variety of ceremonies in which tribal members come together each year during summertime. Their goals were to celebrate the renewal of the universe, which involved fasting and sacrifice, and to seek health and prosperity for their community. The painting above shows another of these ceremonies, the Mandan Buffalo Dance. A more recent ritual adopted by the plains tribes, with significant impact, was the Ghost Dance.

who passed through the prairie on the way to somewhere else, stopping only briefly at trading posts and forts, even though these Anglo-European travelers brought with them diseases that devastated Native American tribes who became exposed to them. But by the middle of the nineteenth century, the whites were passing through in increasing numbers, bringing with them livestock that consumed the prairie grass, and wagons that created rutted trails that disrupted the migrations of the bison. Even worse, many of these settlers were stopping on the plains, carving out homes and farms from the new states and territories

being formed there. Soon towns began to dot the landscape, and railroad and telegraph lines began to connect the towns.

Nowhere was this scenario more evident than in Texas. Formerly a Mexican possession and then an independent state, its vast expanse represented a varied climate and topography. From the lowlands of the east and the central hills, to the buttes and high desert plateaus of the west, Texas attracted settlements, farms, and even plantations in the southeastern part of the state. But the greatest impact on the Indians was from the large cattle ranches stretching across hundred of acres of

BELOW This photograph, from the Mathew Brady collection, shows a large delegation of Native American chiefs and government officials outside the White House in the mid-1800s. Although these meetings were designed to promote goodwill, the course of federal policy toward disposing more Indian land to settlers was not changing.

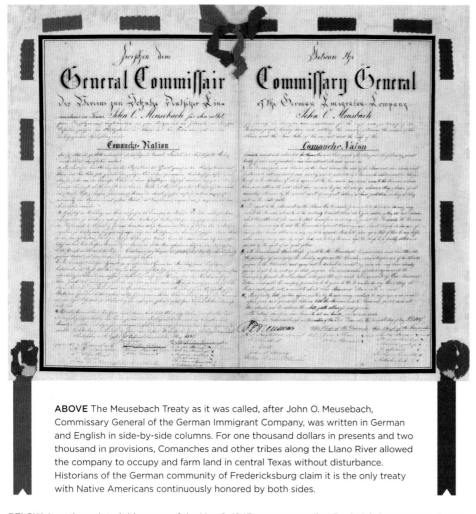

ABOVE The Meusebach Treaty as it was called, after John O. Meusebach, Commissary General of the German Immigrant Company, was written in German and English in side-by-side columns. For one thousand dollars in presents and two thousand in provisions, Comanches and other tribes along the Llano River allowed the company to occupy and farm land in central Texas without disturbance. Historians of the German community of Fredericksburg claim it is the only treaty with Native Americans continuously honored by both sides.

BELOW A settler painted this scene of the May 9, 1847, peace council at Fredericksburg, Texas, during which the Meusebach Treaty was signed by the German Immigrant Company representative, John Meusebach, and war chiefs of the Comanche and Delaware tribes. The treaty was considered fair at the time but the expansion of settlers to the Lone Star state destroyed Comanche hunting grounds.

central and west Texas. The Comanches and the Kiowa, along with another tribe that adopted the plains lifestyle, the Kiowa Apaches, had come down from the mountains in pre-contact times and developed into skilled bison hunters. The Comanches and Kiowas were dominant in the southern plains, just as the Lakota and Cheyenne were to the north.

It became obvious to these tribes in Texas and elsewhere in the plains that they needed to retaliate against the impact on their hunting by the white settlers. Cattle rustling and raids became prevalent. The ranchers were already locked in a struggle with farmers—whom they termed "sod busters"—who were cutting into their grazing land. The disturbances caused by the Indians aggravated an already tense situation. Law enforcement agencies, vigilante groups, and soldiers went after Indian war parties and settlements.

The isolated incidents of raids and massacres on both sides escalated into a full-scale frontier war. For example, in 1835, a special militia, the Texas Rangers, was formed to fight Indians while the Texas regulars were battling the Mexican Army. Besides traditional weapons and tactics, the Indians used firearms (traded or stolen) to augment their warring capabilities. Liquor enhanced or supplanted traditional spiritual ideals of invincibility. But the firepower and organization of the forces ranged against them were too great to allow the Native Americans more than transitory victories. The frontier war would continue with tragic results for the white, but more especially for the Native American populations, for the remainder of the century.

INDIAN TERRITORY IN 1888

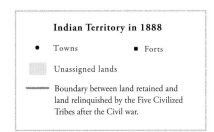

Indian Territory in 1888

- Towns
- Forts

Unassigned lands

Boundary between land retained and land relinquished by the Five Civilized Tribes after the Civil war.

BELOW A lantern slide diagram, shown here in an enlarged form, of the Battle of Seattle. Unrest came to the Pacific Northwest in the 1840s as increased American settlement of Indian lands occurred in the new Oregon Territory, present-day Washington, Oregon, and parts of Idaho. Lechi, an aggressive leader, organized attacks on white settlers and militia patrols in the Puget Sound. One of these attacks, the Battle of Seattle, on 26 January 1856, was between Indians armed with muskets and settlers and militia in the fortified settlement of Seattle, aided by the gunboat *Decatur* on Puget Sound.

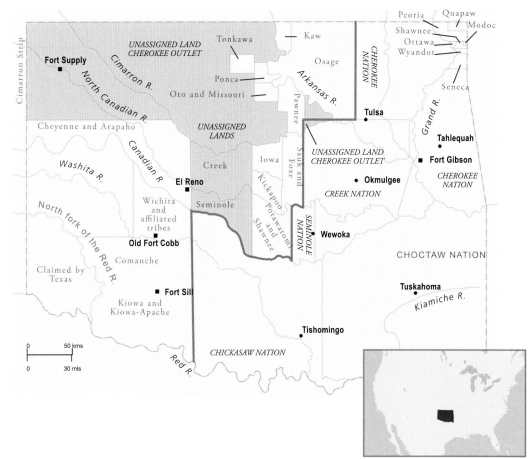

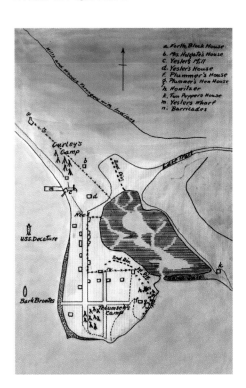

MANHOOD RITUALS

Native American men in virtually every tribe prove their manhood in hunting and warfare. But individual tribes have other traditions. Many cultures use sweat-houses in which men spend time for spiritual enlightenment, camaraderie, and cleansing. The transition to manhood during puberty is treated in some cultures by isolating and/ or drugging the boy in an attempt to induce visions, or subjecting him to the tests and tutelage of elders. The most grotesque manhood rituals are those used by the Plains tribes that involve bodily mutilation. The most common of these is the suspension of the body by skewers through the breast as part of the Sun Dance.

LAST OF THE GREAT WARRIORS: DAKOTA & OTHER PLAINS TRIBES

SCATTERED RAIDS BY THE DAKOTA, NAKOTA, LAKOTA, CHEYENNE, AND OTHER TRIBES IN COLORADO, KANSAS, AND WYOMING TERRITORY CAUSED THE FEDERAL GOVERNMENT TO FOCUS MORE ATTENTION ON THE FRONTIER PROBLEM IN THE PERIOD FOLLOWING THE CIVIL WAR.

Prominent veteran officers who remained in the U.S. Army were at the forefront of the military response to Native American raids and attacks. Attacks on settlers led to a retaliatory campaign by Civil War hero Winfield Scott Hancock on the Cheyenne of Kansas and Colorado in 1867. Seeing a robust force of warriors still present among the Teton Sioux (Lakota), who were made up of the Oglala Sioux and other groups, the administration of President Ulysses S. Grant sent the army's top soldier, William T. Sherman, and others in a peace commission to meet with Chief Red Cloud of the Oglala Sioux.

In May 1868, at Fort Laramie, Wyoming, the commissioners agreed to terms with Red Cloud, which included the closure of all army forts along the Powder River. The Indians were granted sanctuary on their sacred hunting ground, the Black Hills, as long as they maintained peace and abided by the treaty. Relative calm came to the area, and the Bozeman Trail through Montana, for six years.

Then word circulated of an important gold find in South Dakota's Black Hills. Miners came to the area, guarded by

ABOVE General William T. Sherman (third from left facing the camera), general-in-chief of the U.S. Army, and other peace commissioners meet in May 1868 with Lakota, Cheyenne, and other chiefs of the northern plains to negotiate an end to hostilities in the region. The result of the meeting was the second Treaty of Fort Laramie.

SITTING BULL

Sitting Bull was a Hunkpapa medicine man who led the Lakota in the latter part of the nineteenth century. He is best known for defeating George Armstrong Custer at the Battle of Little Bighorn in 1876. After the U.S. Army regained control of the area, Sitting Bull fled to Canada with some of his followers. He returned in 1881 and was placed on a reservation, becoming something of a celebrity and even participating in Buffalo Bill Cody's Wild West Show. When the Lakota embraced violence during the Ghost Dance movement, Sitting Bull was killed by Indian police while resisting arrest on December 15, 1890.

OPPOSITE TOP This Henry repeating rifle was presented to the Oglala Sioux chief Sitting Bull the Minor (or the Good) by President Ulysses S. Grant on June 6, 1875. Sitting Bull the Minor was one of the Lakota chiefs who adhered to the terms of the Treaty of Fort Laramie. However he was killed by rival Crow warriors during a hunting expedition on the Tongue River on December 16, 1876.

NOTABLE FORTS, TRAILS & "INDIAN WAR" BATTLES ON THE GREAT PLAINS

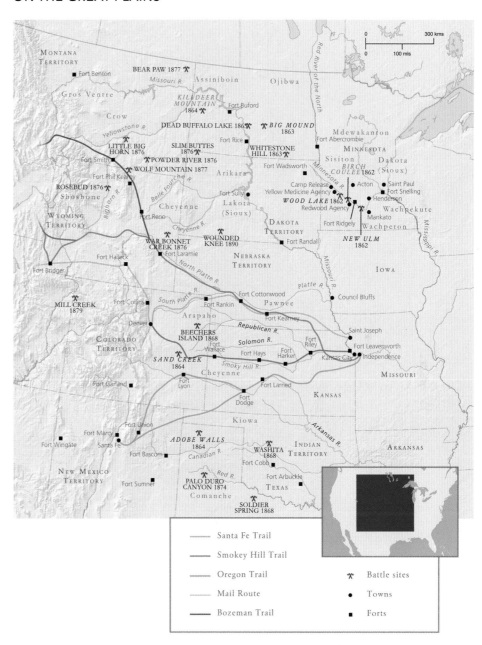

THE MASSACRE OF THE WICHATA,

OR

SHERIDAN'S LAST RIDE.

BY "SHENANDOAH," AUTHOR OF "MOKE-TA-VA-TA," THE MARTYRED CHIEFTAIN.

I.

On the Wichata, at break of day,
The Cheyenne chieftain's village lay—
The remnant small of a mighty band,
Now scattered and torn like the rifted sand;
The wandering winds with warnings woke
The ghosts of his murdered kin, who spoke :
Fly! fly! for the morn bringeth fresh dismay
From Sheridan ninety miles away.

II.

A thousand horsemen, with weapons bright,
In the frore and frosted morning light,
Ride over the snowy-sheeted ground,
With a shuddering, smoldering, sullen sound;
They have seen the tents in the night's cold noon,
And backward rode 'neath the veiled moon,
Prepared to pounce, like a bird of prey,
On the fated village a mile away.

III.

The Indian saw the countless throng,
Like the trees of the forest, many and strong ;
He stood like a hunted hound at bay,
Then sent this message without delay :
"Ye are many and we are few ;
Ye can drink our blood as the sun the dew,
For we have our women and children small,
A hundred and thirteen souls in all ;
My handful of warriors are strong and brave,
They will fight my helpless people to save ;
There is no fear in the chieftain's eye ;
He cannot fight, for he will not lie ;
He came with this pledge only yesterday
From the father ninety miles away."

IV.

No answer came. In another breath
They swept to their wretched work of death,
With a maddening shout and a deafening yell,
Like the dire and dreadful fiends of hell ;
And babes from their mothers' breasts were torn,
And sires were scalped in the light of morn ;
The ground was crimson with their blood,
And the river reddening with its flood ;
Mangled forms lay bleeding and bare,
With a ghostly, ghastly, sickening glare.
And one rode foremost among them all,
Urging them on with shout and call,
On a foaming charger, that seemed to say,
"I have brought you, Custer, all the way,
At the head of a thousand armed men,
With orders traced with a bloody pen,
These trembling mothers and babes to slay,
From Sheridan ninety miles away."

V.

Alas! alas! for the deeds that were done
That day at the rising of the sun !
The tongue shall falter, and pen shall fail,
And lips grow white when they tell the tale
How friend and foe on the field did lie,
All mangled and mingled, to faint and die ;
The victors, panting their fame to spread,
Gave no heed to the dying, no thought to the dead.
Great God! was there none their hands to stay,
With Sheridan ninety miles away ?

VI.

Their cruel and thirsty carnage o'er,
Backward the warriors ride once more ;
They pilfered the lightning from the skies,
And flooded the country with flaming lies,
In these words, blazoned all over the land :
"We have met a hostile Indian band—
Five hundred, counting women and all—
An hundred warriors armed did fall ;
The frontier's safe, for we gained the day,
With Sheridan ninety miles away."

VII.

There was joy in the camp of Sheridan
When his branded minions appeared again,
With their Osage allies, drunken with blood
And the liquid hell-fire's maddening flood,
Came leaping and shouting around the fire
With the gory scalp of the Indian sire ;
Like demons they danced till the dawn of day,
And Sheridan there, not a word to say.

VIII.

The maiden moon took time to unfold
Her silvery bow to a disc of gold,
When Sheridan rode 'neath her shining shield,
Seeking his dead on the bloody field ;
Their souls, like a vapor, before his eyes
Arose, with a shivering, sad surprise,
To show their forms all shrouded in blood.
The prey of the wolves and the vultures' food,
Fifteen days did brave Elliott lay,
And Sheridan ninety miles away.

IX.

All honor to those who, with sword and pen,
Rise up to defend the rights of men ;
Who succor the weak and battle the strong,
Sustaining the right, denouncing the wrong ;
Who would fly the Indian's life to save
From the lawless murderer's conquering glave,
But chiefly honor the glorious three,
The valiant sons of a nation free—
One far in the fiery, flaming South,
Who flew to rescue from death's dark mouth
The hunted few of an Indian band,
When the Texan Rangers were close at hand ;
And him, the special and martyred one,
Whose name now shines like the flaming sun ;
And him, the youngest, whom gold could not buy,
The glorious "white man that would not lie."
These, these would have rushed the carnage to stay
Had they been a thousand miles away.

X.

But for this deed, this one without a name,
Columbia bendeth her forehead in shame ;
And the Angels of God on the plains above,
Pause awhile in their ceaseless work of love,
To gaze, while one with a burning pen
Erases the name of Sheridan,
And carves on the golden scroll of fame,
The story of him with the spotless name—
Moke-ta-va-ta, who dared to die
Rather than basely utter a lie ;
Whose pleading women and children were slain,
In the light of morn on the crimson'd plain,
By a mounted host of merciless men,
Under orders grav'd with a faithless pen,
Making this a 'St. Bartholomew's day,"
And Sheridan ninety miles away.

NOTES.

1. STANZA 1.—*The Cheyenne Chieftain.*—Moke-ta-va-ta, the most remarkable man of the age for magnanimity, generosity, integrity and courage. His hospitality to destitute emigrants and travelers on the plains, for years, had no limit within the utmost extent of his means ; giving liberally of his stores of provisions, clothing and horses. His fame as an orator was widely known ; he was great in council and his word was law. Hundreds of whites are indebted to him for their lives. At Sand Creek, Colorado, in the fall of 1864, while in the employ of our Government and under the protection of its flag, he was attacked, and one hundred and twenty of his men, women and children murdered. On that occasion, with only forty-five warriors, he made an attack unparalleled in history. He held Chivington's seven hundred men at bay for seven hours and carried to a place of safety three hundred of his women and children—twenty of his braves and his own wife pierced with a dozen bullets. Previous to the conflict, after his two brothers had been shot down and cut to pieces before his eyes, (while approaching the troops to notify them of the friendly character of the Indians), he aided three white men to escape from the village, one of them a soldier. They were his guests, whom he suspected of being spies, "but did not know it," and they are now living to the eternal fame and honor of the chieftain. From Sand Creek he fled to the Sioux camp, where it was determined to make war upon the whites in retaliation. He protested against interfering with women and children, and insisted upon fighting the men. He was overruled. Thereupon he resigned his office as chief, and assumed the garb of a brave. He soon after made peace for his tribe, which was faithfully kept until the burning of their village two years afterward. A war again ensued, in which he took no part, having promised never again to raise his hands against the whites. He was the first to meet the Peace Commissioners at Medicine Lodge Creek. His many services and virtues "plead like angels trumpet-tongued against the deep damnation of his taking off."

2. THE SAME.—*His Murdered Kin.*—One hundred and twenty of his men, women and children were assassinated at Sand Creek, and mutilated in the most horrible and disgusting manner. And at Pawnee Fork, two years after, when the Cheyenne village was burned and their property destroyed by "Major General" Hancock, an orphan, an idiotic Indian girl, nine years of age, was outraged and, murdered.

3. STANZA VII.—*Their Osage Allies.*—Osage Indians, who constituted a portion of Sheridan's command, and were employed against the Cheyennes. Even Chivington had a better sense of decency, propriety, or expediency ; for when he started out to destroy Moke-ta-va-ta's village, he declined the proffered services of the Ute Indians, inveterate enemies of the Cheyennes. In this, as well as in the fact that he did not budge an inch from Sand Creek until he had cared for and removed his wounded and dead forty miles to Fort Lyon : he deserves commendation ; for, he "not being the worst, stands in some meed of praise."

4. STANZA VIII.—*Fifteen Days.*—After the attack upon the village, the destruction of life and property, and shooting of hundreds of ponies, the troops marched back to Camp Supply, reporting Major Elliott and seventeen of his men missing, their fate unknown. After waiting fifteen days, the bodies of these men were cared for. Elliott and his men (ignorant of the real character of the Indian village, and disdaining to molest the women and children or property), engaged in a hand-to-hand encounter with the warriors, but not being sustained by the command otherwise employed, were cut off and abandoned.

5. STANZA IX.—*The Glorious Three.*—Major General Geo H. Thomas, who commanded at Camp Cooper, Texas, some ten years ago, made a forced march of an hundred miles, with one hundred and twenty cavalry, to protect a village of Comanches from Baylor and three thousand rangers that were marching to destroy them. General Thomas was successful. He then marched in rear of the Indians hundreds of miles to shield them from the Texans. This gallant and chivalric officer has recently (to the shame and disgrace of the Government) had Sheridan promoted over him.

Major General John Sedgwick, who fell during the war of the rebellion, rendered similar services on the plains, in defence of the Arrapahoes, at about the same time ; and Colonel Edward W. Wynkoop, five years later, in behalf of the Cheyennes. This young officer is often spoken of by the Indians as the "Tall Chief that don't lie."

Other officers might be mentioned for similar services, among them Generals Z. Taylor, W. S. Harney, and Alfred H. Terry. The last mentioned, two years ago, with a strong head, heart, and hand, squelched a conspiracy in Montana to extirminate the Crow Indians. Again, the next summer, flying across the plains, and up the Missouri river as fast as steam could carry him, to rescue a Sioux village from the border settlers. This splendid officer was removed from the command of the Department of Dacota, to make room for the blunderer Hancock.

Capt. Silas S. Soule, in Colorado, a few years ago, and Lieut. Philip A. Sheridan, in Oregon, ten years since, might also be referred to in this connection, as drawing their swords in defence of the Indians and the right.

In the same cause many noble men have used their pens—among them President U. S. Grant, in his recent inaugural ; Hon. George W. Manypenny ; Wendell Phillips, Esq.; and Col. William A. Phillips, of Kansas.

6. STANZA X.—*St. Bartholomew's Day.*—On St. Bartholomew's day, 24th of August, 1572, during the reign of Charles IX, a massacre of the Huguenots took place in Paris, followed by others in the different cities and provinces of France. Thousands were assassinated. Three officers only—Henride Savoic, Governor of Provence ; the Visconut d'Orthez, Governor of Bayonne ; and St. Heran, Governor of Auvergne—refused to obey the orders of the king. At the Sand Creek massacre, before referred to, there were three officers who protested against attacking the Indians—Capt. S. S. Soule, Lieuts Cramer and Baldwin. Capt. Soule was assassinated in Denver, Colorado, for his efforts to save the Indians on the field, and his evidence afterwards. At the massacre of the Wichata there was none to protest—no, not one.

WICHITA MASSACRE (OPPOSITE)

The Massacre of the Wichita (sic) or Sheridan's Last Ride. An author who went by the pen name of Shenandoah wrote this stirring ode to the murder of Chief Black Kettle and raid on his village by the 7th U.S. Cavalry, the Battle of Washita on November 27, 1868. Caught between an unyielding army and young warriors who would not lay down their arms, Black Kettle suffered a second devastating attack on his Cheyennes at the doorstep of sanctuary in the Indian Territory. The poem's author provides extensive footnotes to explain the symbolism of the verse and makes historic references to personalities in the western Indian wars.

FORT LARAMIE TREATY

The first and last pages of the 1868 Treaty of Fort Laramie. Actually the second treaty with this name, it was a compromise similar to the Medicine Lodge Treaty of the previous year between the federal government and the tribes of the southern plains. At Fort Laramie, commissioners led by William T. Sherman agreed to allow the Native Americans a large tract of land in the Black Hills in exchange for an elimination of hostilities and raids and a move toward reservation settlement. Negotiated by lesser chiefs, Red Cloud nevertheless was successful in his demand for the closure of a series of army forts.

an army expedition under George Armstrong Custer. The treaty was violated and a new wave of violence commenced in 1876. Custer and other cavalry commanders, under the overall command of Brigadier General Alfred Terry, battled the Indians in Montana and the Dakotas to force them onto reservations. On June 17, the Lakota scored a major victory over Brigadier General George Crook's forces at the Battle of the Rosebud in Montana Territory. Terry ordered Custer to advance on the Sioux, but to avoid an immediate engagement. Convinced he would be successful in routing an encampment of Oglala Sioux, Cheyenne, and Arapaho under spiritual leader Sitting Bull, Custer took his 7th Cavalry to the Little Bighorn River on June 25, 1876.

There he divided his command into three segments. While Custer's two subordinates failed to gain any advantage, Custer took 210 men toward the camp from the east. At the Little Bighorn, warriors under Crazy Horse massacred Custer and his men, scalping them and leaving no soldiers to survive. The rest of the 7th was pinned down for two days until the Indians broke camp as Terry approached. The war continued for nearly a year. Crazy

Horse surrendered in 1877, but was killed by a guard. By the end of the decade, the surviving Native Americans of the Great Plains had been forced onto smaller reservations. Sitting Bull fled to Canada with some of his people in 1876, then returned four years later and was placed on a reservation.

About this time, a new spiritual phenomenon swept through the Indians on the reservations. The Ghost Dance was a religious philosophy that told of Native Americans being reunited with their dead ancestors, and the return of the earth to the favorable conditions of an earlier time. By 1890, the Teton Dakota had begun disturbances on the reservations, bringing a violent reaction from the white authorities to the spread of the Ghost Dance. Sitting Bull was killed while resisting arrest at Standing Rock Agency in North Dakota during a disturbance associated with the Ghost Dance. After Sitting Bull was killed, Big Foot took control of the Lakota. In December 1890, the army under Major General Nelson A. Miles defeated (many say massacred) Big Foot's band at Wounded Knee Creek in South Dakota, virtually ending resistance by the warriors of the Great Plains tribes.

"They made many promises and only kept one, they promised to take our land and they did."

Chief Red Cloud

LEFT Cheyenne artist Lame Deer illustrated the attack at Little Bighorn on dismounted cavalry troopers by mounted Lakota and Cheyenne warriors on deer hide to commemorate the greatest Native American victory in the western Indian wars.

BIG FOOT

Big Foot was a Lakota chief who was firmly dedicated to the Ghost Dance belief. Shaken by the fate that befell Sitting Bull at Standing Rock, he and his followers fled their homes near the Cheyenne River Agency and headed for the Black Hills. The 7th Cavalry surrounded their camp at Wounded Knee Creek on December 28, 1890. After a tense night, a warrior struggled when soldiers attempted to disarm him and general firing began. Indians fleeing the tipis were shot down, many of them women and children. Big Foot was found later frozen to death and one of the saddest chapters in Native American history came to a close.

LEFT This nineteenth-century color lithograph of the June 25, 1876, Battle of Little Big Horn dramatizes the greatest victory of the Plains Indians over the U.S. Army. The topography was quite different. The five companies of the 7th Cavalry led by Custer were on a plateau east of the river and the allied warriors charged up from the river. There were no tall mountains in the immediate area. Custer was dressed in buckskin that day with his hair cut short.

BELOW This headdress belonging to Crazy Horse was made of the skin and feathers of the red-backed hawk. In addition, he wore into battle a lightning bolt painted across his face and dots representing hail, images that came to him in a vision quest he experienced at an early age.

LAST OF THE GREAT WARRIORS: APACHE & COMANCHE TRIBES

THE COMANCHES, KIOWAS AND KIOWA APACHES SAW THEIR DOMINANCE
OF THE TEXAS PLAINS COME TO AN END DURING THE SECOND HALF
OF THE NINETEENTH CENTURY, BUT THE STRUGGLE RAGED UNTIL 1875.
WHILE OTHER TRIBES OF THE PLAINS WERE MAKING PEACE OR WAR TO
THE NORTH, THESE WARRIORS CONTINUED THEIR RAIDING ON TEXAS
RANCHERS AND SETTLERS, ALTHOUGH WITH DECREASING SUCCESS.

Texas Rangers (the state mounted police force) and Indian fighters drove the Comanche and Kiowa raiders into the panhandle region. The war parties then turned their attention to settlers, stages, and supply trains using the Santa Fe Trail through northern New Mexico.

Northwest Texas and northeastern New Mexico were still subject to Indian raids after the Civil War. The government first tried to negotiate peace treaties. In August 1865, a meeting was arranged to bring together tribes of the region and government negotiators, including Kit Carson, to offer reservation land and limited hunting off the reservations in exchange for peace. The resulting Little Arkansas Treaty was signed on October 14, but the state governments of Texas and Kansas, as well as a society of Cheyenne warriors known as the "Dog Soldiers" refused to recognize the accord. Fighting and raids broke out again in the north. Again, the government tried to negotiate, offering land in Indian Territory taken from those tribes that had sided with

LEFT Quanah Parker was a Quahada Comanche war chief, the son of a white mother kidnapped by the tribe as a girl and a Comanche chieftain. With Quahada war parties, he raided and warred against the army, who respected his leadership. When he finally surrendered, he was a tireless protector of the rights of his people on the reservation, prospered in trade, and supported the Peyote Cult.

COCHISE

Cochise was the leader of the Chokonen Band of Chiricahua Apaches. Like Mangas Colorado and other Apache leaders of the mid-1800s, he led his bands on raids into Mexico, his people's foe over many generations. He did not attack the Americans moving through and into the area around Apache Pass, until the Bascom Affair, in which Cochise was arrested when he went to parlay with an army officer over an allegation of kidnap against the Chiricahua. From then on he waged war against the soldiers—including during the Battle of Apache Pass in 1862—until in 1871 he was forced onto the Chiricahua Reservation where, three years later, he died.

the Confederacy. The Treaty of Medicine Lodge in 1867 brought together many tribes, but some warriors continued raiding, even as other chiefs led groups of their followers toward the new reservations.

Major General Philip Sheridan formed three columns to converge on the recalcitrant tribes and drive them onto the reservations. Overcoming resistance from the warriors as he went, by 1869 Sheridan had got most of the southern Plains Indians onto reservations. There were some tragedies along the way, such as George Custer's senseless massacre of Cheyennes at Washita in November 1868. But renegade bands led by the Quahada Comanches—who signed no treaties—continued to attack whites. A new Kiowa leader, Satanta, emerged to join them. He led warriors on raids against the Texans even while living on the reservation. In May 1871, he was arrested in a confrontation with General W.T. Sherman at Fort Sill, was tried and imprisoned.

The Quahada, under their chief Quanah Parker, remained on the rampage for another four years, fighting white hunters who competed with them for the shrinking

ABOVE Chiricahua Apache prisoners, including in the first row Chief Naiche, center, and Geronimo, second from right, were photographed in a stop during their rail transfer from Fort Bowie, Arizona, to confinement at Fort Marion, St. Augustine, Florida. Geronimo, Naiche, and another chief, Chihuahua, surrendered their bands to the U.S. Army on September 4, 1886.

LEFT This photograph is of "Naches" or "Wei-chi-ti" (Naiche), the Chiricahua Apache chief who was the son of Cochise. He is pictured with his wife and is holding a rifle. He was imprisoned for a time at Fort Marion with Geronimo and other Apache leaders.

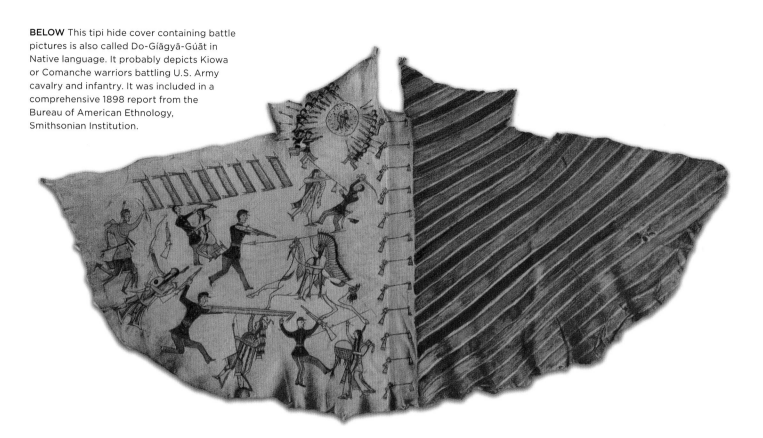

BELOW This tipi hide cover containing battle pictures is also called Do-Gíägyä-Gúät in Native language. It probably depicts Kiowa or Comanche warriors battling U.S. Army cavalry and infantry. It was included in a comprehensive 1898 report from the Bureau of American Ethnology, Smithsonian Institution.

bison herds. After Indian fighters resisted an attack by Quanah's warriors near Adobe Walls in 1874, 5,000 Kiowa, Cheyenne, and Comanche people fled the reservation, fearing retaliation. They followed the Red River west, taking refuge in the deep canyons of the area. However the U.S. Cavalry pursued them, and in late September, they were dealt a serious blow when troopers under Colonel Ranald Mackenzie discovered and destroyed a large camp at Palo Duro Canyon. The last of the surviving refugees were forced back onto the reservation by the spring of 1875, and individual leaders were banished to a Florida military prison to maintain the peace.

Farther west, another group of Apaches, the Chiricahua, attacked troops and travelers on the roads west, using their homes in the mountains on what is now the Arizona–New Mexico border as a base, and exploiting increased mobility from stolen horses. When the United States acquired the region from Mexico, the Apaches initially made peace with the newcomers. Trouble began when the Americans, bound by treaty, policed Apache raids south into Mexico. During the Civil War, Cochise was detained when the Chiricahua were accused of kidnapping a rancher's son and his confrontation

with Lieutenant George Bascom escalated into bad blood between the army and the Apaches.

Cochise and the Chiricahuas finally submitted to settlement on a reservation southeast of Fort Bowie. But after the old warrior died, young Apaches tired of reservation life and resumed marauding and killing. Then in 1876 the government moved them to the more inhospitable San Carlos Reservation in the desert to the west. The unrest grew. From these events emerged Geronimo, the greatest warrior of the southwest, to lead the Chiricahua. Even though he was not a chief, his exemplary courage and fighting spirit inspired many Apaches to wage ferocious raids on the settlers and soldiers of southeastern Arizona. Geronimo took a group of warriors and left the reservation for Mexico. First General George Crook, who had great respect for the Apache fighting ability and spirit, tried to bring Geronimo and his bands to terms in May 1885. But the Chiricahua continued to resist until General Nelson Miles, who had brought about the surrender of several tribes on the northern plains, maneuvered Geronimo into a position where he was forced in September 1886 to surrender, bringing a close to the Native American violence in the southwest.

ABOVE Two men pose with rifles on an Apache rancheria. After the reservation proved not to be satisfactory for teaching the Chiricahuas to increase their use of agriculture in the arid southwest, the government set up smaller rancherias, communal farms where the residents grew hay and other crops for sale and trade.

ABOVE The woodcut illustration on this *Harper's Weekly* cover from April 24, 1886, brought the Apache War into the homes of America. The bottom lithograph is from a photograph of a meeting between General George Crook and Geronimo and other holdout Chiricahua leaders.

ABOVE This rawhide shield with a design of double-ended hooks in blue paint was picked up by an American soldier who fought in the Mexican War. Along with the shield, which has a wooden handle on the back held by leather thongs, is a "potato masher" carved wooden war club. The weapons are believed to be Pima in origin and the design could be Hopi, or influenced by Spanish Basque settlers.

GERONIMO

Goyahkla, "one who yawns," grew up in a peaceful mountainside community of Chiricahua Apaches. After achieving warrior status, Goyahkla alternately raided and traded with the Mexicans. In 1850, while he was away, Mexican soldiers raided his camp, killing his mother, wife, and his three babies. He led a retaliatory raid against them, and from the ferocity of his reaction was thereafter known as Geronimo, derived from the plea for mercy to St. Jerome uttered by his victims. His bravery and tactical skill brought him to the attention of Cochise and Mangas Colorado, whom he fought under. After their deaths, he assumed leadership of the Chiricahua until he and his band were cornered in 1886. Exiled to Fort Marion in Florida, he was then brought to Fort Sill, Oklahoma, where he dictated his memoirs while under house arrest.

ALASKAN & ARCTIC TRIBES MEET THE AGE OF INDUSTRIALIZATION

AS THE TWENTIETH CENTURY BEGAN, THOSE NATIVE AMERICANS LIVING AT THE TOP OF THE WORLD PRESERVED A CULTURE THAT HAD IN MANY WAYS REMAINED UNCHANGED FOR THOUSANDS OF YEARS.

Large-scale contact with whites had been taking place for nearly 150 years, as Russian and British traders established outposts on the coastal and island areas, and then began to establish communities. A greater impact on the Eskimo population occurred through the introduction of their manufactured goods, culture, and religions. But the natives continued to live their lives much as their ancestors had done.

In 1867, the United States purchased Alaska from Russia. Meanwhile, the newly constituted Dominion of Canada,

which had achieved increased autonomy from Great Britain, established its own policies and methods for dealing with the natives. Certain segments of the Eskimo and sub-Arctic Eyak populations began to feel a greater impact from the white influx. Besides the trading communities that grew from the initial outposts, the whites set up whaling and fishing operations with bases in the coastal areas. Then the discovery of gold deposits in Alaska and Canada along the Yukon River in 1897 led to an inrush of prospectors and consequently huge impact on the Native Americans, as the newcomers and their camps encroached on the traditional hunting grounds of the inland sub-arctic groups. By the 1920s, however, the gold deposits were tapped out, and any incidental benefits accrued by the native population ended.

By this time, the Eyak tribe still roamed vast areas of the sub-arctic, continuing their traditions of hunting, gathering, and occasional cultivation, although they were being nudged aside in some areas by Blackfeet and Blood Indians, who had been driven north from their own traditional hunting grounds, and by the white prospectors. The Eskimos, categorized in the twentieth century into three general

LEFT The Miles Brothers photographed two Tlingit women and several children along the Kotsina River, Alaska, in 1902.

TOP LEFT This photograph shows Eskimos harpooning a whale at Point Barrow, Alaska. The animal is at or near expiration so the ceremony of thanksgiving, a time-honored tradition of connection between the spirit of the people and the spirit of the animal, is set to begin.

TOP RIGHT A photograph of a grave in Nome, Alaska, home to the Bering Strait Eskimos. Besides Christian crosses of their adopted faith, Eskimos leave worldly goods at the gravesite, in this case two rifles, for use by the spirit they believe lives on after death.

ABOVE Early twentieth-century Eskimo goggles. Like their ancestors centuries earlier, Inuit of the early twentieth century survived by hunting caribou and other mammals on the tundra and frozen shoreline as well as depending on sea mammals and fish. These goggles helped the Eskimos prevent snow blindness on hunting excursions.

JAPANESE OCCUPATION IN THE ALEUTIAN ISLANDS

During World War II, the Japanese seized the western portion of the Aleutian Islands. Parishes of the Russian Orthodox Church, like this one in the village of Attu, ministered to the spiritual needs of the Aleut villagers during the Japanese occupation and military rule. The presence of the church and the priests gave a sense of stability to the people in a time when, for a period of four years, their world was turned upside down.

groups, the Aleuts, Yupik, and Inuit (Eskimo for "people") found themselves in competition with the new technology of white entrepreneurs for the sea mammals and fish that provided the food and materials for their survival. Even so, the last group of isolated tribesmen of the Arctic Sea, the Copper Eskimos, had never seen a European before 1910.

Gradually, many of the Eskimos and the Eyak adopted the products of modernization, while still holding onto many of their traditional methods and customs. Woolen clothing, rifles, and sail-power entered their lives. While firearms and liquor were officially banned by the governments of the U.S., Canada, and Denmark (which ruled Greenland), they were traded nevertheless, with often devastating and deadly consequences for the native populations. Some natives found work in the mining camps, canneries, steam whaling fleets, and later military installations, of the whites. Others had to compete with them, but found value in the trade of baleen (whalebone) and blubber, until newer technology cut the demand for those products. In the 1920s fox fur was in vogue, but the Great Depression cut the demand. These market fluctuations created a great deal of economic stress for those Native Americans who depended on trade rather than traditional hunting and fishing for survival.

Shortly before World War II, the governments of the U.S. and Canada began to formulate national policies for their northern native populations, a development the Danish government had undertaken years earlier in Greenland. Schools and medical facilities followed in the wake of those the missionaries had established long before.

ABOVE LEFT Ola, a beautiful Noatak woman, poses with her husband and child. The expressive faces of the Arctic people relay the natural goodness and joy of life that emanates from deep inside them.

ABOVE Simiguluk, an Eskimo spear and lance maker at Point Barrow, Alaska, proudly displays some of his handiwork to photographer Stanley Morgan in 1935.

THE MODERN ARCTIC HUNTER

Hunting and fishing still play important roles in the lives of many Eskimos. Seals, whales, polar bears, fish, game birds, and other animals are still pursued, whether for commercial sale or personal consumption. The modern hunter often uses technology to his advantage. Snowmobiles, fiberglass kayaks, motorized canoes, harpoon guns, and winches have often replaced traditional man- and dog-power, animal-skin disguises, weapons with wooden shafts, and sealskin boats. However some hunters still occasionally use age-tested tools and methods. Eskimos still take part in traditional ceremonies to bring bountiful harvests, engage in competitions to keep their bodies in shape, and perform rituals to release the souls of their prey.

But with government organization and aid came regulation, especially laws regarding wildlife exploitation and land conservation. For the Native Americans of the north, these ideas were foreign to their cultural traditions which allowed the taking only of what they needed and the caring for the spirits of their animal prey. Gradually, the blend of old and new meshed, but the discovery of oil in 1968 along Alaska's Prudhoe Bay brought a new round of struggles between the original inhabitants and the governments who sought to impose their own rules.

ABOVE RIGHT This 1927 photograph shows a group of Inupiat kayakers at Noatak, Alaska. Their double-ended paddles are shown at the ready on calm waters, but the Eskimos can dig them into the brine at a moment's notice, turning on the spot and swiftly pursuing prey.

RIGHT Knik Chief Nikaly and his family are pictured in a 1910 photograph taken near Anchorage, Alaska, by H. G. Kaiser.

ALLOTMENT & REFORM:
NATIVE AMERICANS ENTER
THE TWENTIETH CENTURY

THE LAST PART OF THE NINETEENTH CENTURY SAW A MAJOR SHIFT IN THE
WAY THE UNITED STATES GOVERNMENT VIEWED THE NATIVE AMERICAN
POPULATION. THIS CHANGE CAME ABOUT AS A RESULT OF THE DAWES
ACT, A PIECE OF LEGISLATION SPONSORED BY SENATOR HENRY DAWES
OF MASSACHUSETTS AND PASSED BY CONGRESS ON FEBRUARY 8, 1887.

Proponents argued that Native Americans should have an opportunity to own farm land individually, just as white Americans had. They argued that many Native Americans were taking on the ways of whites, and should therefore be treated equally. The land was taken from breaking up the old reservations into sections. Each head of household would receive 120 acres, with half that amount doled out to single persons and orphans, and 30 acres to non-orphans under 18 years of age.

Like most of the federal government's strategies for dealing with the Indians, the Dawes Act had a dual purpose. Besides attempting to modernize the treatment of Indians by treating them as individuals, it was also an attempt to gain more land for—and avoid friction as a result of— the land rushes of the 1890s. This was especially true in Indian Territory, where whites were greedily eyeing Native American tribal reservations. The eventual result was the largest single-day land grab in American history and the formation of the state of Oklahoma. There were exceptions: the reservations of the Five Civilized Tribes and the other long-established tribes of Indian Territory, the Seneca Reservation in New York, and a portion of northwest Nebraska below the Dakota Reservation were exempt from the parceling, at least under the initial law.

LEFT Chief Yellow Bear poses with his daughter at the Carlisle Indian Industrial School at the turn of the century. The school was founded in 1879 by former U.S. Army officer Richard Henry Pratt, who had first practiced his rehabilitation theories on Apache and Arapaho warriors imprisoned at Fort Marion in Florida.

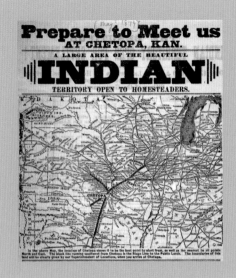

FROM INDIAN TERRITORY TO OKLAHOMA

Oklahoma derives its name from the Choctaw words "okla" meaning people and "homa" meaning red. The Indian Territory had been established by the U.S. Congress in the 1830s, but the passage of the Homestead Act in 1862 was a catalyst for an increasing influx of settlers from the 1870s, beginning in the sparsely settled panhandle region. Court decisions paved the way for opening lands to white settlement and the passage of the Dawes Act opened non-tribal lands for survey. President Benjamin Harrison opened two million acres for settlement and the first land run occurred on April 22, 1889. Later settlement was conducted by lottery, and in 1907 the territory became a state.

LEFT This handbill from May 1879 was designed to attract people to tour land in the Indian Territory. The advertisement claims to offer land not part of any designated reservation. This bill appeared ten years before the Indian and Oklahoma (panhandle region) areas of present-day Oklahoma were opened to homesteading.

ABOVE Coach Glenn Warner (standing back row, center) is pictured with the 1912 track and field team of the Carlisle Indian School. Warner accompanied two members of the team, Jim Thorpe and Hopi long-distance runner Louis Tewanima, as their coach to the 1912 Olympics in Stockholm, Sweden.

ABOVE RIGHT A Navajo silversmith displays his wares and tools in this 1880 photograph. Turning traditional crafts into a cottage industry appealing to tourists was a major part of tribal adjustment entering the twentieth century.

RIGHT A Potawatomie woman weaves outside a reservation dwelling.

DAWES ACT

The idea behind the legislation known as the General Allotment or Dawes Act was to assimilate Native Americans into the general population, thereby relieving the burden of the federal government to care for them. But the law was deficient in quite a few areas. Even those Indians who did take to individual farming lacked, in most cases, the knowledge, tools, seeds, and especially the quality of soil that successful white farmers had. Problems of qualification and inheritance were abundant and cheating was rampant. The policy started by the Dawes Act led to the even more controversial policy of termination.

separate and apart from any tribe of Indians therein, and has adopted the habits of civilized life, is hereby declared to be a citizen of the United States, and is entitled to all the rights, privileges, and immunities of such citizens, whether said Indian has been or not, by birth or otherwise, a member of any tribe of Indians within the territorial limits of the United States without in any manner impairing or otherwise affecting the right of any such Indian to tribal or other property.

Sec. 7. That in cases where the use of water for irrigation is necessary to render the lands within any Indian reservation available for agricultural purposes, the Secretary of the Interior be, and he is hereby, authorized to prescribe such rules and regulations as he may deem necessary to secure a just and equal distribution thereof among the Indians residing upon any such reservations; and no other appropriation or grant of water by any riparian proprietor shall be authorized or permitted to the damage of any other riparian proprietor.

Sec. 8. That the provisions of this act shall not extend to the territory occupied by the Cherokees, Creeks, Choctaws, Chickasaws, Seminoles and Osage, Miamies and Peorias, and Sacs and Foxes, in the Indian Territory, nor to any of the reservations of the Seneca Nation of New York Indians in the State of New York, nor to that strip of territory in the State of Nebraska adjoining the Sioux Nation on the south added by Executive order.

Sec. 9. That for the purpose of making the surveys and resurveys mentioned in section two of this act, there be, and hereby is, appropriated, out of any moneys in the Treasury not otherwise appropriated, the sum of one hundred thousand dollars, to be repaid proportionately out of the proceeds of the sales of such land as may ———— be acquired from the Indians under the provisions of this act.

Sec. 10. That nothing in this act contained shall be so construed as to affect the right and power of Congress to grant the right of way through any lands granted to an Indian, or a tribe of Indians, for railroads or other highways, or telegraph lines, for the public use, or to condemn such lands to public uses, upon making just compensation.

Sec. 11. That nothing in this act shall be so construed as to prevent the removal of the Southern Ute Indians from their present reservation in Southwestern Colorado to a new reservation by and with the consent of a majority of the adult male members of said tribe.

Approved February 8, 1887

Grover Cleveland

John G. Carlisle
Speaker of the House of Representatives.

John Sherman
President of the Senate pro tempore.

The plan was not without its problems and the Bureau of Indian Affairs had a difficult time implementing it. The determination of who was eligible for the land was complicated by the existence of many people of mixed blood. Once the allotments were determined, tribal governments were to be abolished and the Indians were to recognize only federal and state laws. Not only were many Native Americans unfamiliar with individual farming, but a fair number resisted the notion. Of those who were willing, few had the capital to invest in stock and equipment. Many of the allotments in the west, moreover, were in arid areas unsuitable for farming. There were no clear-cut provisions for passing the land on to heirs, and the allotments of deceased heads of households were divided up into small parcels among their heirs.

Many of those minors who received allotments did so while they were away from their tribes and families attending government boarding schools. Like the schools established earlier by Christian missionaries, the Indian schools were designed to integrate the coming generations of Native Americans into the general population, but without the religious indoctrination of missionary endeavors. The first federal Indian school was established on a military reservation in south central Pennsylvania at Carlisle in 1879. Other schools were established by the federal and state governments around the nation. They did serve the purpose of educating many Native Americans, and raised literacy gave them valuable life skills and prepared some to go on to higher education, sports, and artistic opportunities. But critics argued the students suffered a loss of connection with their tribal roots. In some cases, this was true, in others a mix of Euro-American education was balanced with respect for tradition.

About this time a new non-governmental reform movment was beginning to be heard as well. Seeing the plight of the Indians forced onto increasingly smaller tracts of land, and with government stipends often keeping them in destitution, reformers generated a public outcry for better treatment of America's original habitants. It would be many years before the movement had significant impact. However, as bad as the situation was in the United States, the Dominion of Canada waited another 50 years to implement a central policy to assist their Native American cultures in adapting to the rapid changes that modernization and technology handed them in the twentieth century.

TOP Indian police remove members of the Cupertino band of Mission Indians from the sprawling Warner's Ranch in northeast San Diego County to Pala, further north. The removal in 1903 was one of the last forced relocations of Indians within the United States. Even though the band settled the new land successfully, it did not erase the pain of being forced off lands considered home.

ABOVE This 1872 photograph is of a Chippewa settlement in the Great Lakes region of Canada and prominently features several wigwams or tipis.

EDUCATION AND CITIZENSHIP

Cherokee parents in the early nineteenth century encouraged their children to learn English to help them deal with the influx of English-speaking whites. Ever since then, Native American education has gone through fits and starts. The Indian boarding schools, which for a century were at the forefront of assimilation, gave way by the 1950s to schools on reservations. From the Land Allotment Act, Indians were given citizenship when deemed competent to handle their own affairs, increasing the importance of education. The Citizenship Act of 1924 made citizens of all native-born Indians, but with the government still in control of their affairs. Canadian Native Americans were given the status of British subjects in the nineteenth century, but were likewise restricted by government regulation of their affairs.

ABOVE This crayon and pencil drawing by Hunkpapa Sioux Joseph No Two Horns is entitled *Tatanka Notanka*. This artwork was created around 1900 and the scene is documented to have appeared on No Two Horns' tipi.

ABOVE One of the most enduring forms of communication among the Plains tribes of North America was pictographic accounts drawn on bison hides and tipi walls. This 1909 bison robe by Blackfeet tribesman Running Rabbit portrays stories of hunting and combat.

⬥ECLARATION·OF·ALLEGIANCE
TO·THE
GOVERNMENT·OF·THE·UNITED·STATES
BY·THE
NORTH·AMERICAN·INDIAN

We, the undersigned representatives of various Indian tribes of the United States, through our presence and the part we have taken in the inauguration of this Memorial to our people, renew our allegiance to the Glorious Flag of the United States, and offer our hearts to our Country's service. We greatly appreciate the honor and privilege extended by our white brothers who have recognized us by inviting us to participate in the ceremonies on this historical occasion.

The Indian is fast losing his identity in the face of the great wave of Caucasian civilization which are extending to the four winds of this Country, and we want fuller knowledge in order that we may take our places in the civilization which surrounds us.

Though a conquered race, with our right hands extended in brotherly love and our left hand holding the Pipe of Peace we hereby bury all past ill feeling and proclaim abroad to all the nations of the world our firm allegiance to this Nation and to the Stars and Stripes, and declare that henceforth and forever in all walks of life and every field of endeavor we shall be as brothers, strive hand in hand, and will return to our people and tell them the story of this memorial and urge upon their their continued allegiance to our common Country.

Joseph Packinian

P Renti   avv

White man Runs King
Medicine Crow

Two moons

Red Hawk
Edward Hoven

Shoulderblade

Red Cloud

Beg man

Dlage Wolf

Little Wolf

Black Wolf
Wooden Leg

Milton Whiteman

Willis Rowland

John P. Young

Reuben Estes

Henry Leeds

Reginald Oshkosh

Robt. Summer Yellowtail
Many Chiefs
Chapman Schanandoah

Richard Wallace

Frank Shively

Lewis Beer

Angas P McD malie

Tennyson Berry

Mitchell Mountain

Peter Demonie

Delos K. Lonewolf

I hereby attest that this document was inscribed by the Indians herein named, on the hill top of Fort Wadsworth, the Site of the National Indian memorial, on the Twenty Second February nineteen thirteen

President of the United States

Wm H Taft

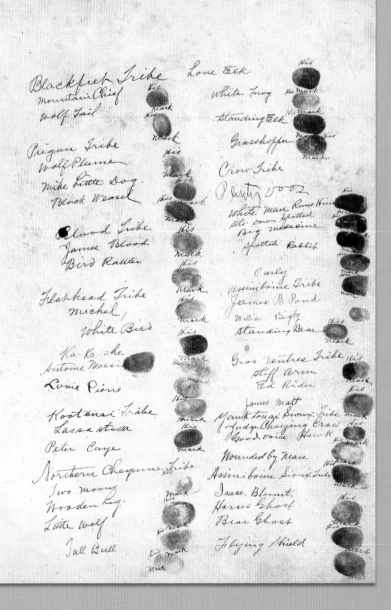

WANNAMAKER TREATY

The Declaration of Allegiance of all Indian tribes was a remarkable document that grew out of a 1909 grand council of Native American chiefs in which harmony among Indians and between Indians and others in American society was emphasized. The declaration was presented to those chiefs present at the 1913 dedication of a National Indian Memorial in New York harbor. Federal officials then entrusted the document to Rodman Wanamaker, the department store magnate, who went on a voluntary 27,000 mile journey around the United States, adding 157 to the 32 original signatures on the declaration. A sample of those 189 signatures, which represented every major tribe, is presented here.

THE NEW DEAL, REORGANIZATION & TERMINATION

BY THE 1930S, CANADA HAD CAUGHT UP WITH THE UNITED STATES IN THE PROCESS OF SETTING ASIDE LAND FOR ITS INDIAN TRIBES, AND INDEED WENT ON TO SURPASS HER SOUTHERN NEIGHBOR IN THIS REGARD. THE UNITED STATES, HAVING COMMITTED 130 MILLION ACRES OF LAND FOR NATIVE AMERICANS IN 1887 AS A RESULT OF THE DAWES ACT, SAW THAT NUMBER SHRINK TO 44 MILLION ACRES BY 1933.

In the midst of the social reforms spurred by the Great Depression and the election of Franklin D. Roosevelt as U.S. President in 1932, the Bureau of Indian Affairs also gained a new reform-minded director, John Collier. He immediately set about changing government policies toward those Indians on reservations.

ABOVE An Apache farmer operates a mule-driven plow on the sandy soil of southern Arizona.

Central to his strategy was organizing and empowering the tribal councils on the reservations in their dealing with the government. He engineered congressional passage of the Wheeler–Howard Act on June 18, 1934, which contained a great number of the reforms he envisioned. The act, known as the Indian Reorganization Act when enacted, permitted the tribes to form constitutions and charters and negotiate with the B.I.A. with the force of a united group. Collier took steps to improve food, medical, and growing conditions on the reservations and started an Indian branch of the Civilian Conservation Corps, one of the New Deal work programs. More Native Americans were placed on the B.I.A. payroll and exempted from civil service rules that might have denied them the jobs. Critics of these programs pointed out that not all Native American were ready for the kind of autonomous status the New Deal proponents were willing to dole out, either on an individual or a tribal level.

There was truth in what they said. The former Plains tribes had not adapted well to farming, and continued to survive largely on government rations and annuities. Of the tribes that did adopt constitutions or charters, many simply used the B.I.A. guidelines and failed to incorporate provisions that would gain acceptance among traditionalists in the tribe. For their part, state and local governments did not generally favor

UNITED STATES AND CANADIAN POLICIES

The United States and Canada adopted different emphases in their policies toward their Native American populations. The population of Canadian Indians was less numerous and spread over a wider area. Reservations (reserves) existed in Canada, but did not pose the kind of challenges experienced south of the border. The early recognition of Canadian Indians as British subjects and a non-politicized Indian Bureau gave the appearance that Canada's policy was more fair. But the Canadians had similar problems in settling their Plains tribes and did not welcome refugees from the United States, such as the Dakota and Lakota. Later in the century, policies fell into a kind of lockstep with the U.S., though the Canadians' failed experiment with termination lasted until 1969.

RIGHT This photograph is of delegates to a convention of Indian Affairs for all California reservations which took place at Riverside, California, in 1930. At the time, the former Mission Indians were struggling to make the desert lands allotted to them into viable reservation communities while the tribes in the northern part of the state were laboring to make their subsistence on rancherias and losing members to urban areas.

BELOW RIGHT Pisehedwin, a Potawatomie Indian, and others gather in front of his Kansas farm home in 1877. Under the Dawes Act individual farming parcels were cut from reservation land. Unlike this tidy farm, most parcels were on lands difficult for even experienced agriculturalists to work.

the repurchase of lands for the tribes, and many found ways to hold up the federal repurchases on behalf of the Indians. In one of the more controversial but necessary provisions of the act, a "blood quantum system" was established to identify who was a member of a tribe and could therefore qualify for loans and aid. Those who were full or half-blood natives, as well as family members who resided on the reservations at the time the act passed, met the blood quantum test.

One of the positive measures of the New Deal policies was in the formation of rancherias—a Spanish term for the tribal livestock ranches that sprung up in the west. A livestock reduction plan and other conservation measures aimed at raising prices of livestock was put in place. In Minnesota, Montana, North and South Dakota, and Arizona particularly, the purchase of additional lands for the tribes went smoothly and credit extension for the purchase of livestock, seed, and equipment opened up great opportunities for tribes in those areas.

ABOVE These Seminole men are training to fight forest fires in Florida. Many Native Americans joined the U.S. Forest Service as firefighters in the second part of the twentieth century.

ABOVE TOP Havasupai men proudly display watermelons grown during the 1950 harvest. The Havasupai adapted to farming well on the irrigated lands of northern and western Arizona.

ABOVE Cherokees living in Cherokee North Carolina in 1952. Thanks to the efforts of a white nineteenth-century store clerk named William Holland Thomas, a band of Cherokees who lived in the Great Smoky Mountains of western North Carolina were able to remain on their native lands after removal of the rest of the Cherokee Nation to Indian Territory. Thomas became a lawyer and lobbied for protection of the tribe's rights under an 1819 treaty before the state government of North Carolina and the U.S. Congress.

The value per head of the tribes' stock rose, profits accumulated, and loans were repaid. Programs like 4-H clubs and other youth and family organizations encouraged a sense of cohesion and contributed to the success of the ranches. The New Deal did not cure all the problems that kept many Native Americans in poverty and depression during the time of cultural assimilation, but it was a start.

With the onset of World War II, the government moved into a wartime mode. The B.I.A. was transferred to Chicago, employees left or were reassigned, funds were cut, and Japanese-Americans were interned on some reservations. A great number of Native Americans left the reservations to join the armed forces or work in war factories. After Roosevelt's death in 1945, Collier was replaced as the head of the B.I.A. With the post-war economic and population boom, politicians questioned the continued need for federal control of Indian affairs. They now saw assimilation as a realistic goal. More Native Americans were moving to the cities voluntarily or through government-sponsored relocations. Indians and non-Native Americans—for varying motives—

MODERN RESERVATIONS AND RESERVES

Map labels:
Lummi, Makah, Swinomish, Quinault, Nisqually, Grand Ronde, Warm Springs (Paiute, Tenino, Wasco), Former Klamath, Fort Bidwell, Hoopa Valley (Yurok), Round Valley, Pyramid Lake (Paiute), Tule River, Fort Mojave and Chemehuevi Valley, Chamash, Colorado River Mohave, Kumeyaay Bands, Fort Yuma (Quechan), Cocopah, Colville, Spokane, Blackfoot, Kalispel, Coeur d'Alene, Yakima, Nez Percé, Flathead (Flathead, Kutenai), Umatilla (Umatilla, Cayuse, Walla Walla, Paiute), Fort McDermitt, Duck River (Paiute, Shoshoni), Walker River (Paiute), Former Uintah & Ouray (partly terminated), Kaibab (Paiute), Havasupai, Hualapai, Hopi, Papago, Maricopa, San Xavier (Papago), San Carlos (Apache), Gila River (Pima), Zuni, Acoma, Fort Apache, Navaho, Ute Mountain, Southern Ute, Jicarilla (Apache), Taos, United Pueblos 19, Canoncito (Navaho), Isleta (Pueblo), Laguna (Pueblo), Mescalero (Apache), Sarcee, Rocky Boy (Chippewa, Cree), Fort Belknap (Gros Ventre), Fort Peck (Sioux, Assiniboine), Northern Cheyenne, Fort Berthold (Arikara, Gros Ventre Mandan), Crow, Cheyenne River (Sioux), Lower Brule (Sioux), Standing Rock (Sioux), Wind River (Northern Arapaho, Shoshoni), Pine Ridge (Sioux), Rosebud Sioux, Santee Sioux, Turtle Mountain (Chippewa), Devil's Lake (Sioux), Red Lake (Chippewa), Nett Lake (Chippewa), Leech Lake (Chippewa), Crow Creek (Sioux), Yankton Sioux, Ponca, Sisseton Sioux, Osage, Omaha, Winnebago, Kickapoo, Iowa, Potawatomi, Sauk and Fox, White Earth (Chippewa), Menominee, Bay Mills, Menominee and Stockbridge, Oneida, Isabella (Chippewa), Chippewa, Kahnawake, Mohawk, Penobscot, Onondaga, Tuscarora, Seneca, Pequot, Shinnecock and Poospatuck, Eastern Cherokee, Alabama & Coushatta, Ctiimacha, Choctaw, Brighton, Big Cypress, Everglades, Mikasuki

Scale: 0 — 500 KMS / 0 — 300 MLS

lined up on both sides of the argument for "Termination": the emancipation of all Native Americans from federal stewardship. Though House Resolution 108, passed in 1953, officially began the termination policy, it was carried out in piecemeal.

Two of the initial tribes to experience the effects of termination were the Klamaths of Oregon and the Menominees of Wisconsin. The Klamaths underwent termination, pushed by Indians already living off the reservations, in return for per capita payments laid out in the "Termination" plan. However, many recipients mismanaged their money and the tribe remained in a state of widespread poverty. The Menominee tribe attempted to manage its affairs in the form of a private corporation, but state and local taxation, resource exploitation by outsiders, and a breakdown of services caused the enterprise to fail. Few clear-cut advantages came out of "Termination" and although it dragged into the 1960s, the federal government then turned again to the B.I.A. and new solutions to the problems of the Native American population.

CIVILIAN CONSERVATION CORPS—INDIAN DIVISION

Roosevelt's New Deal policies had their greatest impact in programs aimed to raise the economic status of poorer Americans. Government-created jobs in public works had the dual benefits of an immediate income for the workers and a lasting legacy of improvements to infrastructure. Many Native Americans received opportunities through the C.C.C.—I.D. (Civilian Conservation Corps—Indian Division). As well as finding work for Native Americans as unskilled laborers on roads, public buildings, and forest conservation, a dedicated effort was made to unleash their artistic talents in creating works of art. These could be producing individual paintings or craft projects in educational settings where the more experienced guided the beginners, or creating paintings, murals, and other works that celebrated Native American heritage.

FIGHTING ON THE OTHER SIDE: NATIVE AMERICAN SOLDIERS

NATIVE AMERICANS HAD FOUGHT ALONGSIDE WHITE FORCES DURING THE FRENCH AND INDIAN, REVOLUTIONARY, 1812, AND CIVIL WARS. BUT FROM THE TWENTIETH CENTURY, NATIVE AMERICANS NO LONGER FOUGHT ON THE BATTLEFIELD TO RETAIN OR REGAIN THEIR LAND THOUGH THE FIGHT CONTINUED IN THE COURTS.

ABOVE LEFT Private First Class Ira Hayes at age 19, ready to jump at the Marine Corps Paratroop School in 1943. He was one of the five Marines in the Iwo Jima flag-raising photograph. A reluctant celebrity after the war, he appeared as himself in the 1949 film *Sands of Iwo Jima* with John Wayne.

ABOVE RIGHT Three WWII Marine Corps women reservists were photographed at Camp Lejeune, North Carolina, on October 16, 1943. They are, from left to right, Minnie Spotted Wolf, a Blackfoot, Celia Mix, Pottawatomie, and Viola Eastman, Chippewa.

Most were living, happily or unhappily, on reservations, or were forced to abandon their culture and integrate with the majority of non-natives in search of work. Opportunities for economic advancement were rare for Indians, most of whom were, at the turn of the century, just beginning to deal with the trauma of assimilation. It is easy to understand why, therefore, when the United States became embroiled in World War I, Native Americans enlisted in large numbers in the armed services. Young men, restricted from carrying out their traditional roles as hunters and warriors on the reservations, longed for the adventure and opportunity military service would bring. However, these young men's enthusiasm for enlistment was not always shared by their families and tribal elders. This was particularly true among those tribes that only a generation or two earlier had been battling the U.S. Army on their homelands.

Those who returned from World War I as veterans tended to be drawn to urban areas. With the military cutbacks made by the U.S. after World War I, few Indians remained in the service, but were forced instead to seek out what jobs they could find in the urban areas and port cities where they were discharged. Others returned, somewhat discouraged, to the reservations after their brief experience of assimilation. There is no evidence to suggest that Native Americans were victims of racial prejudice in World War I any more than were African Americans. In the

GENERAL CLARENCE L. TINKER

General Clarence L. Tinker, born in Oklahoma, was the son of George Edward Tinker, Sr. and Sarah Ann "Nan" Schwagerty. He was of Osage lineage and already a distinguished airman by the time the United States entered World War II. A two-star general, Tinker was commander of Hickam Air Force Base in Honolulu. After the success of the Doolittle Raid, Tinker planned an ambitious raid on Japanese-controlled Wake Island. He ordered four long-range bombers for the attack. After being outfitted and flown to Hawaii, the planes were readied for the mission. The first attempt to bomb the island was scrubbed due to bad weather and Tinker's plane was lost at sea. But the rest of the squadron returned to Wake Island in late June 1942 and carried out a highly successful raid, the first made at a range of more than 1,000 miles from base. The flyers had fulfilled Tinker's dream.

RIGHT The Pulitzer Prize-winning photograph of the raising of the American flag on Mount Suribachi during the battle of Iwo Jima by Associated Press photographer Joe Rosenthal. At the left of the picture is Ira Hayes, a Pima, along with Franklin Sousley, John Bradley, Harlon Block, Michael Strank, and Rene Gagnon. All but Bradley, a Navy corpsman, were U.S. Marines. Hayes, Bradley, and Gagnon survived the fight.

trenches of the European war, the man next to you was your best friend and protector no matter what his race.

During World War II, many more Native Americans answered the call of duty—a greater proportion, in fact, of their number than that of the general population. Tribal resistance to military service was no longer a major factor, as veterans of the previous war had, on the whole, benefited from their experience. Native Americans joined every branch of the U.S. Armed Services. Eskimos and Eyaks from Canada joined the Royal Navy, Army, and Air Corps alongside other Canadians. While some Native Americans were victims of racial discrimination in training camps—from stereotyping jokes to hazing—these actions and attitudes changed when the soldiers, sailors, airmen, and marines were sent overseas. As in World War I, American and Canadians of differing skin colors united in their fight against a common enemy.

RIGHT WWII bomber pilot Lieutenant Woody J. Cochran displays a captured Japanese flag in this photograph taken on New Guinea, April 1, 1943. A Cherokee from Oklahoma, Cochran earned the Silver Star, Purple Heart, Distinguished Flying Cross, and Air Medal.

BELOW A group of Native American U.S. Marines pose with their rifles during a World War II training exercise.

CODE TALKERS

"Code Talkers" was the nickname of those soldiers, members of the U.S. Navy and Marines, who used Native American languages to code transmissions and military dispatches, as a result denying vital information to the enemy. Although the largest and most famous group was the Navajo code talkers of World War II, Native American code talkers of various tribes had used their historic languages to baffle enemy interceptors during the two world wars. The code talkers of World War II acted as, or with, radio operators, confusing enemy listening posts and keeping the Allies' vital military dispatches secret.

RIGHT Corporal George Miner, a member of the Winnebago tribe from Tomah, Wisconsin, poses for a U.S. Army Signal Corps photographer while on guard duty in 1919 at Niederähren, Germany at the end of World War I.

MIDDLE RIGHT U.S. Army Lieutenant Ernest Childers, a Creek, is congratulated by General Jacob L. Devers in 1944 after receiving the Congressional Medal of Honor in Italy for wiping out two machine-gun nests.

FAR RIGHT Tobias William Frazier was a Choctaw from Oklahoma and served as a U.S. Army code talker in World War I.

At home, Native Americans got involved in the war effort in various ways. Women, or those too old to serve, worked in defense plants or provided support services to those who did. Women Native Americans also joined the Womens' Army Corps (W.A.C.S.) and Women Accepted for Voluntary Emergency Service (W.A.V.E.S.) Others participated in civil defense teams. The extreme northern part of the continent was closer than any other part of North America to the air bases Germany was placing in Norway, Denmark, and Poland. The development of radar allowed the Allies to build an early-warning system with stations along the Arctic Circle. Many Canadian and Alaskan Eskimos worked in building and maintaining these stations. They would, during the Cold War a decade later, help construct the North American Aereospace Defense Command (N.O.R.A.D.) defense.

The heroics of Native Americans in World War II are too numerous to detail here, from Louie Adrian, a Spokane Indian who died fighting on Suribachi, to Walter Lawyer, a chief's descendant who served and died in Germany in 1945, and Tommy Prince, the most decorated Canadian of aboriginal descent. Native Americans have fought in Korea, Vietnam, and all the subsequent conflicts involving American troops. The stories mentioned here are dedicated to all Native Americans, living or dead, who served their two countries in the name of freedom.

Sub-Course No. 4   WIRE TIES AND SPLICES   5 Hours

LESSON NO.	SCOPE	TEXT REFERENCE	M of I

1	WIRE TIES
	  MARLIN TIE
	  BASKET WEAVE TIE
	  KNOB TIE
	  SQUARE KNOT TIE
	  CLOVE HITCH
	
	Demonstration and explanation by instructor followed by application by student.
	
	Trng. Aids: Short Lengths W-110.
		FM 24-5
		Technique of
		Field Wire
		Systems.
			C
			D
			A

2	WIRE SPLICES
	  SQUARE KNOT WITH SEIZING WIRE
	  SQUARE KNOT WITHOUT SEIZING WIRE
	  T SPLICE
	  WESTERN UNION SPLICE
	
	Demonstration and explanation by instructor followed by application by student.
	
	Trng. Aids: TE-33 per man, seizing wire, rubber tape, friction tape, W-110 and W-130.
		FM 24-5
		Technique of
		Field Wire
		Systems.
			C
			D
			A

3-5	PRACTICE SPLICING AND MAKING TIES All students will be required to practice splices and ties until proficient. Instructors will assist students and grade splices and ties. Trng. Aids: TE-33 per man, seizing wire, rubber and friction tape, W-110, and W-130.		A

Sub-Course No. 3   NAVAJO VOCABULARY   40 Hours

LESSON NO.	SCOPE	TEXT REFERENCE	M of I
1-25	NAVAJO-ENGLISH VOCABULARY NOTE: This is a course in pure memory work. It is instruction in a syllabus of English words most frequently used for communications in the Marine Corps and learning exact equivalents in the Navajo language. The student learns by constant repetitions and drill.	Navajo Dictionary.	C D A
26-40	MESSAGE TRANSMISSION IN NAVAJO In this phase of instruction the students will send prepared messages over telephone nets in Navajo with the receiving party translating to the English equivalent. A careful check must be made by the instructor to ascertain that the message is an exact translation of the prepared message. Trng. Aids: Message Book per man, pencil, Navajo Dictionary, EE-8 telephones, W-130, prepared traffic. NOTE: The prepared traffic must be so worded as to cause the usage of new words learned from the Navajo Dictionary.	Navajo Dictionary.	C D A

Sub-Course No. 2   NAVAJO ALPHABET   15 Hours

LESSON NO.	SCOPE	TEXT REFERENCE	M of I
1-15	MEMORIZING NAVAJO ALPHABET Explanation of function and use of Navajo Alphabet. Oral drill in memorizing Navajo words representing English letters. Written and oral drills on Navajo Alphabet. Transmission of short messages in Navajo. Trng. Aids: Navajo Dictionary, paper, pencils, blackboard, P.A. System, EE-8 telephones, W-130.	Navajo Dictionary	C D A

FIELD SIGNAL BATTALION
SPECIALIST TRAINING REGIMENT, MARINE TRAINING COMMAND
SAN DIEGO AREA, CAMP PENDLETON, OCEANSIDE, CALIFORNIA.

1 February, 1945.

MASTER SCHEDULE
NAVAJO TALKERS COURSE
(4 weeks)

1.	Printing and Message Writing.	10
2.	Navajo Alphabet.	15
3.	Navajo Vocabulary.	40
4.	Wire Ties and Splices.	5
5.	Wire Laying.	5
6.	Pole Climbing.	5
7.	Telephone and Switchboard Operation.	5
8.	Voice Procedure.	10
9.	Message Center Operation and Procedure.	10
10.	Navajo Message Transmission.	30
11.	SCR-300-500.	20
12.	TBX.	16
13.	Organization of Infantry Regiment.	5
	TOTAL HOURS...	176

NAVAJO TALKERS COURSE

SUB-COURSE 8   VOICE PROCEDURE   10 HOURS

LESSON NO.	SCOPE	TEXT REF	M OF I
1	INTRODUCTION TO VOICE PROCEDURE	FM 24-9	C D
	TRNG AIDS P.A. SYSTEM, BLACKBOARD		
2	CALL SIGNS AND COMPONENT PARTS OF MESSAGE FM 24-9		C D
	TRNG AIDS: P.A. SYSTEM, BLACKBOARD		
3	PROCEDURE PHRASES	FM 24-9	C D A
	TRNG AIDS: P.A. SYSTEM, BLACKBOARD, EE-8 TELEPHONES, W-130		
4	PROCEDURE PHRASES	FM 24-9	C D A
	TRNG AIDS: P.A. SYSTEM, BLACKBOARD, EE-8 TELEPHONE, W-130		
5	MICROPHONE TECHNIQUE		C D
	TRNG AIDS: P.A. SYSTEM; ALL TYPES OF MICROPHONES, TF 11-2061		
6-10	PRACTICE VOICE NETS		D A
	TRNG AIDS: P.A. SYSTEM, MSG BOOK PER MAN, PENCIL EE-8 TELEPHONES, W-130, CANNED TRAFFIC.		

NAVAJO TALKERS COURSE

SUB-COURSE NO 1   PRINTING AND MESSAGE WRITING   10 HOURS

LESSON	SCOPE	TEXT REF	M OF I
1	INTRODUCTION TO COURSE. CORRECT METHOD OF PRINTING LETTERS AND NUMBERS	FM 24-5, PAR 33	C D
	TRNG AIDS: LETTERING CHARTS, BLACKBOARD, PAPER, PENCILS.		
2-3	PRINTING, (APPLICATION)	FM 24-5, PAR 33	D A
	TRNG AIDS: LETTERING CHARTS, BLACKBOARD, PAPER, PENCILS		
4	DESCRIPTION AND USE OF MESSAGE BOOK	FM 24-5, PAR 38 NAVMC-3589, SECT 3	C D
	TRNG AIDS: ENLARGED MSG BLANK, BLACKBOARD, MSG BOOK PER MAN, PENCILS		
5-7	WRITING OF MESSAGES (PRACTICAL APPLICATION)	FM 24-5, PAR 38 NAVMC-3589 SECT 3	C A
	TRNG AIDS: MSG BOOK PER MAN, PENCILS, TEXT FOR PRACTICE MESSAGES		
8	USE OF AUTHORIZED ABBREVIATIONS	FM 24-5, PAR 35 NAVMC-3589, SECT 4	C A
	TRNG AIDS: BLACKBOARD, MSG BOOK PER MAN, PENCILS, MIMEO "LIST OF AUTH. ABBREVIATIONS".		
9	THE PHONETIC ALPHABET	FM 24-5, PAR 176	C D A
	TRNG AIDS: P.A. SYSTEM, MIMEO "PHONETIC ALPHABET", BLACKBOARD		
10	USE OF TELEPHONE IN TRANSMITTING MSGS		D A
	TRNG AIDS: EE-8 TELEPHONES, W-130 WIRE P.A. SYSTEM, MSG BOOK PER MAN, PENCILS, MIMEO "TEXT FOR PRACTICE MESSAGES"		

NAVAJO DECODE DOCUMENT

Confidential documents that describe course work, including lessons for the use of the Navajo alphabet, its application to the transmission of secret wartime communications, and radio operator field duties in the training of Navajo code talkers in the U.S. Marine Corps, 1945.

URBAN MIGRATION OF NATIVE AMERICANS

THE TRANSITION OF NATIVE AMERICANS FROM THE CAMPS AND COMMUNITIES OF THEIR HOMELAND, TO RESERVATIONS, AND THEN FINALLY TO THE CITIES OF AMERICA, WAS A LONG JOURNEY AND PRIOR TO THE 1930S, ONE MADE BY VERY FEW INDIANS.

ABOVE (From left) Ironworkers John Tionekate Scott, Peter Atawakon Rice, Jim Ross, Adrian Bonnelly (non-native lawyer), Joe Tehonate Albany, Paul Kanento Diabo, and Dominic Otseteken McComber were all involved in Diabo's successful 1927 challenge to U. S.-Canadian border crossing restrictions in U. S. District Court under the provisions of the 1794 Jay Treaty.

Unlike African Americans who, after gaining their freedom as a result of the Union victory in the Civil War, flocked to the cities in large numbers in search of new opportunities and a better life, few American Indians saw cities in the same light. Indeed, the Dawes Act encouraged them to become farmers, tilling their own plots of land. The majority who did not take advantage of the program remained on the reservations, practicing traditional lifestyles, and seeing their

IRONWORKERS

One group of Native Americans established a lasting reputation for their special skills. These were Mohawk men whose bravery and agility made them ideally suited for work on large building and civil construction projects. From a beginning as unskilled laborers on a bridge across the St. Lawrence River in Quebec, they spread out over the continent working on high steel bridge and building construction, including during the boom in steel-girder skyscrapers that sprang up in New York during the 1920s. The demand for their skills was so great that they frequently crossed the U.S.-Canadian border to practice their craft. After the tragedy of September 11, 2001, Native American ironworkers who had built the World Trade Center returned to advise officials on how it was constructed.

LEFT Kahnawake Mohawk ironworkers Frank White, Julian Decaire, Angus Leclaire, Bill Meloche, Mack Montour, Joe Canadian, and friends pose for a picture on a high steel project.

affairs managed by the Bureau of Indian Affairs. There were, however, exceptions. Those Native Americans who attended public and private Indian boarding schools and learned new skills or continued into higher education were more liable to end up in cities than their fellow tribesmen. Those who excelled in adapting to the ways of the whites traveled to those places where their skills and knowledge were in demand— in industry, education, medicine, sports. Others gained opportunities and position by intermarriage. Most of these openings were typically available in or near the large cities.

Though the Mohawks and other Native American ironworkers succeeded in keeping the typical wages of Native American workers in the cities above the national average, some were not so fortunate. The lack of education forced many to accept low-paying jobs and they suffered from prejudice, particularly in the American northwest. Those who had a history of alcoholism or arrest could not land permanent employment. Often they were only employed in seasonal work or day labor. When they did get government jobs, they would find themselves in unfamiliar territory when those jobs ended. Many drifted back to the reservations.

Then in the 1950s, the U.S. government changed policy abruptly, and began to encourage more migration as part of

ABOVE Kidd Smith, a Seneca woodcarver, at work in the Tonawanda Community House in western New York State in 1940. The Seneca and other New York tribes have maintained small reservation lands in the state.

ABOVE Joseph J. Jocks, a Kahnawake Mohawk, rivets a girder on the San Francisco Bay Bridge in the 1930s. The ironworkers traveled North America and even overseas to work on high steel projects.

ABOVE John Howe, a Washoe, poses in front of a furnace in the early 1900s when coal furnaces were stoked by hand. Industrialization and transportation began to replace agriculture and mining as the economic driving force in the American West toward the end of the nineteenth century.

the move towards termination of federal involvement in Indian affairs. Among the reasons for this about-face were the admission by the B.I.A. that the allotment policy was not working and the more insidious desire by corporate and other interests to exploit the reservations for natural resources. Added to the pressure for jobs by returning veterans, the forced migration to the cities left many Native Americans unprepared for the change. Most ended up in the ghettos and Indian bars with little hope of self-improvement.

In the 1960s, the B.I.A. began to implement much-needed changes. They began from within, by bringing more Native Americans to work for the agency. Then, the director and the field officers made sure that federal training and education programs, such as the C.E.T.A. program of the 1970s, were applied to Native Americans in the cities. The B.I.A.

ADAM FORTUNATE EAGLE—PIONEER URBAN LEADER

Adam Fortunate Eagle Nordwall has been a major force in shaping Native American progress and perceptions for over 40 years. Born in Minnesota to a Swedish father and Chippewa mother, he was sent to Pipestone Indian Training School at an early age. He exhibited an interest in art, but settled on starting a small business in San Leandro, California. He became concerned about the trauma experienced by Indians who were driven into cities without the ability to adapt. He was instrumental in starting intertribal support organizations in the San Francisco Bay area. He became a prominent leader statewide and was invited to Washington to give the Native American perspective as the Lyndon B. Johnson administration launched the "War on Poverty" in 1964.

ABOVE TOP Three teenagers in front of the Intertribal Friendship House in Oakland in 1972. The intertribal centers welcomed individuals and families of Native American heritage without judgment.

ABOVE Thomas Benyagka (right) holding the Hopi Prophecy with Bill Wapepah while Dennis Banks looks on at the Intertribal Friendship House, Oakland, California, in 1979. For many years, the intertribal centers were the only safe public places for Native Americans to gather in the cities to talk, exchange ideas, and observe the ceremonies of their heritage.

ABOVE This poster from the 1940s encouraged Native Americans to leave the reservation behind and start a new life working in the burgeoning community of Denver. The campaign was part of a move by the Bureau of Indian Affairs to draw Native Americans off the reservations and into the workforce. It met with limited success.

also made sure that they monitored federal and state education and assistance programs to ensure they met the special needs of the Native American population. Native American opportunities and prosperity increased in urban areas and toward the end of the twentieth century roughly 45 percent of the Native American population in North America lived in or near cities.

OUTSTANDING NATIVE AMERICANS

SINGLING OUT INDIVIDUALS FROM A GROUP, SUCH AS THOSE
NATIVE AMERICANS FEATURED HERE, IS A RISKY PROPOSITION.
THE BREADTH OF THEIR INDIVIDUAL ACHIEVEMENTS CANNOT
BE ADEQUATELY DESCRIBED ON THESE PAGES.

Also, these individuals must be seen only as examples of many more Native Americans in recent years who have achieved public success and personal goals within or partially removed from their cultural heritage. All of those mentioned here have attained great public success, and bring a sense of pride and accomplishment to their people.

One of the early scholars of Native American descent to chronicle Indian culture from a historical perspective was Joseph Matthews, an Osage from Oklahoma. He studied at Oxford

ABOVE Joseph Matthews, author, Osage councilor, and Rhodes Scholar, pictured at his Oklahoma home.

University, was a Rhodes Scholar, and served for eight years on the Osage tribal council. He wrote five books including a massive work on his tribe, The Osages, Children of the Middle Waters, which included research based on documents and interviews with long-time tribal members. His work was not limited to Native American studies. He also penned *Life and Death of An Oilman, the Career of E.W. Marland.*

Oklahoma-born Allie Reynolds was a Creek who showed a talent for pitching early in life. The right-handed pitcher, nicknamed "Superchief," came up through the Yankee organization and served at the major league level in baseball in the late 1940s and early 1950s. He earned 131 victories and was only recently passed by Andy Pettite for ninth place on the Yankee's all-time win list. He pitched in four World Series under Casey Stengal and threw two no-hitters, the only Yankee pitcher to do so, including one in the 1951 play-off run against Boston.

Maria Tallchief, an Osage, was prima ballerina for the prestigious New York City Ballet from 1947 to 1960. She received the "Woman of the Year Award" in 1953 from President Eisenhower and was named "Wa-Xthe-Thonba" or "Woman of Two Standards" by the Osage Tribal Council. She retired from the stage but continues to direct ballet for the Chicago Lyric Opera. Russell "Big Chief" Moore, a Pima Indian, was a fixture in the New York jazz scene of the 1950s and 60s. He played trombone behind Billie Holiday, Louis Armstrong, and many others.

JIM THORPE

Jacobus Franciscus "Jim" Thorpe was born in Indian Territory in 1887. His parents were both half-blood Indians but his mother was a descendant of Sauk-Fox Chief Black Hawk and he was raised in that tradition. Jim Thorpe was a medal winner in the 1912 Olympics in the pentathlon and decathlon, although his medals were taken away when it was discovered he had earlier played some minor league baseball. He later played major league baseball and played and coached for the Canton, Ohio, football team, an original team in the National Football League (N.F.L.) He went on to play in 52 N.F.L. games. His Olympic medals were later reinstated and presented to his children in 1983.

Buffy Sainte-Marie was one of the most popular folk singers of the 1960s and one who changed contemporary perspectives about the appearance of an Indian maiden. In her numerous early concert tours, she sang and played guitar in jeans, boots, and cotton shirts. Only later did she sometimes appear in costume attributed to her roots as a Canadian Cree. Her popularity as a singer-songwriter gained world appeal and her song "Until It's Time for You to Go" was recorded by Elvis, Cher, and Barbra Streisand. She produced 18 albums including compilations and earned several Grammys and an Oscar. In recent years she has been involved in educational interests as well—she has a doctoral degree in education—and has worked with the television program Sesame Street, tribal groups, and her own youth foundation.

Another Grammy winner is Mary Youngblood. Trained as a classical flutist, she earned the award for "Beneath the Raven Moon," one of several disks she has produced with the six-hole Native flute. She continues to work as a performer, composer, and

DEDICATION
Will Rogers
FIELD
OKLAHOMA CITY
JUNE 28, 1941

WILL ROGERS

William Penn Adair "Will" Rogers was born in 1879 on Dog Iron Ranch in Indian Territory to parents of Cherokee heritage. Always in love with cowboy culture, he developed a trick roping act and performed in Florenz Ziegfeld's Follies in New York, adding a comic patter that soon made him one of the show's most popular performers. He obtained roles in silent films, and then went to Hollywood, becoming one of the most popular movie stars, and, at the height of the Great Depression, an influential performer and columnist in radio and print. An avid early supporter of aviation, he died in a plane crash at Point Barrow, Alaska, on August 15, 1935, and was much mourned by a shocked nation.

educator. Likewise, Native American performer Wayne Newton has touched the lives of millions for decades.

Waneek Horn-Miller was assistant captain of the Canadian water polo team at the 2000 Olympics and remains active in Canadian athletics today. She has a deep appreciation for the accomplishments of Native American Olympians who came before her: "Alwyn Morris, 1984 Olympic kayak gold medalist, was the first Canadian aboriginal gold medal winner and is a Mohawk from my community. Sharon and Shirley Firth, Dene Native Americans from the Northwest Territories, are three-time Olympians in cross-country skiing. Billy Mills, 1964 ten-kilometer runner, won the only gold medal in track and field that year for the U.S. He's a Sioux from Pine Ridge, South Dakota."

The only Native American to serve in the United States Senate is Ben Nighthorse Campbell. He was born in Oklahoma but enlisted early in the services and later relocated to Colorado. An injury forced an end to his career in international competitive judo and he became interested in politics. He served in the Colorado General Assembly, the U.S. House of Representatives and two terms as one of Colorado's U.S. Senators, retiring in 2005.

ABOVE Waneek Horn-Miller, who graduated from Carlton University in 1999 with a political science degree, has won medals in numerous Canadian amateur competitions in addition to representing her country at the 2000 Sydney Olympics.

ABOVE Brian Trottier, born in Saskatchewan to a Cree/Chippewa father, was a former National Hockey League Rookie of the Year. He holds many personal scoring records and helped the New York Islanders to win four Stanley Cups in 1980–84.

ABOVE Amazing pitcher Allie Reynolds pictured in New York Yankee pinstripes on his 1954 trading card.

ABOVE Two-term United States Senator from Colorado, Ben Nighthorse Campbell.

OPPOSITE Buffy Saint-Marie performs at a National Aeronautics and Space Administration (NASA) event. Another popular Native American Grammy winner is Robbie Robertson of The Band.

NATIVE AMERICAN ART & LITERATURE

AT THE BEGINNING OF THE TWENTIETH CENTURY THE EMERGENCE
OF INDIAN SCHOOLS—THOSE ON THE RESERVATIONS AND THE
LONGER-ESTABLISHED BOARDING SCHOOLS—GAVE RISE TO AN
INCREASED NUMBER OF NATIVE AMERICANS LITERATE IN THE
ENGLISH LANGUAGE AND VERSED IN A BROAD ARRAY OF CULTURES.

As a result, Native American authors have produced a prolific body of literature over the past century. Whether in fiction, social commentary, or scholarly or spiritual works, they have competed on an equal basis with authors of other races. Likewise, a New Deal era emphasis on art

ABOVE A collage by Arthur Amiotte. In this work the artist combines his own hand-drawn Native American caricatures with scenes appearing in a French journal.

and crafts sparked a renaissance in traditional methods and a transition to broader artistic expression among Indian artists. Native Americans are often portrayed as serious in dramatic productions but they like to laugh. Often, Native American authors and artists cannot help but poke fun or write serious criticism about how the race is perceived by others. The general unfamiliarity with detailed history combined with the stereotyping of Native Americans in popular media has given a skewed view of their culture. The film *Smoke Signals* (1998) achieved great acclaim for its exploration of this theme. Many other Indian artists and writers look at how they are perceived and how they see themselves. This sort of biting commentary is evident in David Bradley's painting *American Indian Gothic* (1983). Bradley is of Chippewa and Lakota descent.

Though he often uses humor in his public expressions on the condition of Native Americans, Adam Fortunate Eagle takes his art seriously. After learning the art of pipe-making he studied art techniques at Haskell Institute under muralist Franklin Gritts, and sculptor and muralist Allen Houser. His sculptures are legendary. But sometimes his sense of humor works its way into his art, as in his installation art statement a tire lodge on a Paiute-Shoshone Reservation. Another Native American artist who possesses the talent to capture a sense of history is Indian Joe Morris. Morris was a longshoreman in San Francisco during the occupation of Alcatraz Island by

R. C. GORMAN

R. C. Gorman is a Navajo artist who has been compared to Picasso for his stylized drawings and prints. His early works in the 1980s and '90s were renditions of Navajo blankets, but he quickly turned his attention to drawing Indian female nudes, a major portion of his body of work. In later years, after having gained acclaim for his drawings, he studied under master printer José Sanchez in Mexico City and added a series of prints, known as the Indian "madonnas," to his expanding collection of internationally acclaimed works. He died in 2005 while still a very prolific artist.

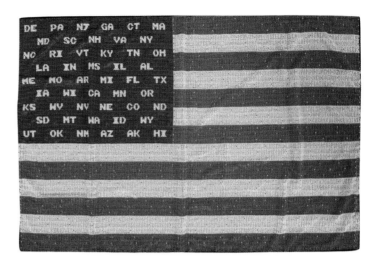

TOP RIGHT Jenny Ann "Chapoose" Taylor, a member of the Uintah tribe of Utah, created this American flag using 130,910 glass beads sewn onto leather with nylon thread. The 23 x 33 inch (58 x 85 cm) work displays the names of tribes of the United States in the stripes and state abbreviations as the stars.

ABOVE *American Indian Gothic*, a lithograph on paper by David Bradley is of course a parody of the famous Grant Wood painting, *American Gothic*. Realizing that "Indians are, by definition, political beings," Bradley decided to make a satiric comment on corruption of Indian values in the art world with the 1983 work.

ABOVE *The Seeing*, a public art sculpture by Johnny Bear Contreras for the Poway, California City Hall, is the result of the artist's interpretation of the transition from the physical world to the spiritual realm.

Native Americans. He sought support for the occupiers from his union and received unanimous approval. His unusual paintings use the materials around which he worked while helping to load supply boats for the occupiers.

Native American artists work in all media. A number of them work with some degree of traditional Indian craft forms. Jenny Ann "Chapoose" Taylor created an American flag entirely from beads in 2002. It is on display at the Smithsonian National Museum of the American Indian on the National Mall in Washington. The museum also features the work of Melissa Cody, an award-winning young Navajo weaver.

Arthur Amiotte is a Lakota artist who was born on the Pine Ridge Reservation and is a descendant of Chief Standing Bear. A studied artist and teacher, he now specializes in collages, using family and public images in combination with his drawings and written narrative. He often includes ledger-book drawings, a traditional form of Lakota art of the nineteenth century, and uses the automobile as a frequent metaphor for his themes of contrasting conditions.

Native American artists often mix traditional and modern themes in works of pottery, basketry, and hide and feather creations. The same is true of writers, both of poetry and prose, who celebrate Native American culture using themes and characters from the past and present. The immense spiritualism of the culture is evident in many works. America Meredith, an upcoming artist, sees her works negotiating the interactions between humans, animals, plants, and spirits. She also likes to explore the space between Native and non-native, being of Cherokee, Swedish, and Celtic descent. "Instead of documenting cross-cultural conflicts, I am interested in portraying those Native and European Americans who could find common ground," she says. Her award-winning work also includes Cherokee symbolism, such as characters from the unique Cherokee alphabet.

Award-winning young sculptor Johnny Bear Contreras, a member of California's Kumeyaay tribe, finds satisfaction in creating public art. He has created stirring works for the cities of Poway and Santa Fe Springs, California, and the Cathedral of Our Lady of the Angels in Los Angeles. His flowing, dynamic style is a reflection of his life transitions, from his youth on the San Pasqual Reservation, via the development of his talent through a combination of formal training and working in the building trades to support his family, and finally to his status as a sought-after sculptor. He reflects on the philosophy that drives his vision: "Often times man can be moving like liquid, or sedentary like stone. He may be slumped on the steps that society has placed before him or he might have created the steps on which he will fall. The steps might also be for advancement."

ABOVE A buffalo sculpture by Adam Fortunate Eagle, who began his artistic endeavors by carving native pipes. He then expressed his natural talent through delicate carvings of animals followed by public and installation art pieces that use satire and humor to make political statements.

ABOVE *Shadow of the Sun* is a tabletop sculpture by Contreras, one of a group that the Sycuan Band of Kumeyaay Indians commissioned him to produce for their hotel property in downtown San Diego, the U.S. Grant Hotel. The historic hotel reopened its doors on October 17, 2006, with Contreras' work on display.

"I long for the day when Native American is a description of the literary work and not the deciding definition."

Sherman Alexie, 2007

ABOVE The acrylic painting *Samonia, Me, and Archie Sam* by America Meredith was inspired by a family friend who had a positive influence on the artist as she was growing up. The three figures in the picture are the artist, her sister, and the family friend, Archie Sam.

LEFT *Richard Oakes, "First" Leader "Killed"* is a painting by Indian Joe Morris. Morris, a member of the Blackfeet tribe, was working the San Francisco wharves when the "Indians of All Tribes" took over Alcatraz Island. Morris was instrumental in keeping the occupiers supplied. He was also a treasurer of the movement and chronicled the occupation through paintings on discarded plywood, including this one of the movement's first leader, Richard Oakes, whose young daughter died in an accident on the island during the occupation.

Indian artists now enjoy the acceptance of a worldwide audience. The works of painters, sculptors, photographers, and muralists are displayed in public buildings, museums, and galleries throughout the world. An annual Native American film and video festival brings together animation, documentary, dramatic, and short subject creations produced by Indian masters of the audio-visual arts. When many of these new works are introduced to the public, whether fine artworks, craft renditions, written word, performances, or filmed entertainment, the Native American creators are involved in a dual function—celebrating the creative interpretation of their heritage while also cementing the contribution of Native Americans to the worlds of contemporary art and literature.

SHERMAN ALEXIE

Sherman J. Alexie, Jr. was born in 1966 on a reservation in Wellpinit, Washington, 50 miles (80 km) from Spokane, and is a Spokane/Coeur d'Alene Indian. Seizures and other side effects of hydrocephaly as an infant kept him something of a loner, but he avidly pursued knowledge and attended Gonzaga University and Washington State, where he received his degree and encouragement in poetry writing. He won several awards for his poetry, wrote short stories for *The Atlantic Monthly* and published a novel. A film based on his work, *Smoke Signals*, won several awards at the 1998 Sundance Film Festival and was commercially released. Today, he is a well known critic, humorist, and television personality in the Seattle area.

TRIBAL LEADERSHIP TRANSITIONS INTO THE TWENTY-FIRST CENTURY

THE LARGE-SCALE ACTIVISM THAT SWEPT THE UNITED STATES AND CANADA IN THE 1960S AND '70S (AS A RESULT OF CONTINUING RACIAL STRIFE AND OPPOSITION TO THE WAR IN VIETNAM) GAVE RISE TO A COUNTER-CULTURE THAT CROSSED A NUMBER OF DEMOGRAPHIC LINES, FROM URBAN AFRICAN AMERICANS TO COLLEGE STUDENTS, CATHOLIC CLERGY, AND OTHERS.

Native Americans, primarily those who were educated and grew up during the period of assimilation following World War II, saw the massive unrest as an opportunity to demonstrate against government policies and racial stereotyping. In November 1969, after years of serious attempts to take over the former federal penitentiary for Indian use failed, a group of Native Americans seized Alcatraz Island in San Francisco harbor and occupied it for 19 months. They offered to "buy" the island for 24 dollars in order to establish a Native American culture and education center there. As occurred with other counter-culture demonstrations, the dramatic and visible action brought the occupants international news attention. The demonstrators held press conferences and maintained

LEFT The San Pasqual Fire Department maintains fire prevention and control programs in addition to being ready to deal with any emergency on the reservation in the arid hills of northeast San Diego County.

ABOVE LEFT The fire station of the Mashantucket Pequot Indian Reservation in eastern Connecticut. The fire department is one of the community services maintained, in large part, from income derived from the resort-casino operations.

ADAM FORTUNATE EAGLE—ACTIVIST

Of his role in the occupation of the vacant Alcatraz Federal Penitentiary in 1969, Adam Fortunate Eagle said, "I discovered the power of the media." He viewed later Native American protests as prone to backlash. "I learned the power of making my points with humor and satire." While some Native Americans critics accused the "Sacred Clown" of embarrassing his people, most have supported his sincere and successful efforts to raise awareness of Native Americans in the eyes of the public. Today Adam Fortunate Eagle, an "elder statesman of modern Indians," writes and creates artworks on a Paiute-Shoshone Reservation in northern Nevada.

an organized colony of men, women, and children on the island. The government was hesitant to use force to evict the Indians, even though many critics called for it.

The demonstrators had many supporters as well among the general population of the Bay area and beyond. Sympathetic groups, including one co-chaired by then State Representative Dianne Feinstein, helped organize supply missions to those occupying the island. Celebrities made appearances and gave speeches on "the Rock." Over time the number of demonstrators on Alcatraz diminished and the last Indians were removed by U.S. Marshals on June 11, 1971. At first the occupation did not appear to be a clear-cut victory for Native Americans, but it soon became evident that public awareness of their demands had been raised.

ABOVE The Mashantucket Pequot Museum is a fine example of recent architectural design and a dynamic repository of Native American culture. The museum and archive contains a large collection of documents and artifacts, many relating to tribes of New England and the northeast. Interactive programs are designed with families and school groups in mind.

LEFT Indian occupiers of Alcatraz waiting to greet new arrivals to the island. The "Indians of All Tribes," as the occupiers referred to themselves, came from many parts of the U.S. and Canada, and most were students. They held the island from November 10, 1969, until U.S. Marshals removed the last 15 occupiers on June 11, 1971.

Shortly before the 1972 U.S. presidential elections, a group of activists organized by the American Indian Movement (A.I.M.) caravanned to Washington, D.C., seeking to have a list of 20 grievances addressed. After being largely ignored in the face of the publicity surrounding the Watergate break-in and other election-year issues, they occupied the Bureau of Indian Affairs (B.I.A.) building and vandalized the offices before a compromise allowed them to leave peacefully. Other occupations took place across the nation as well. Congress reacted to the incident by allowing the Federal Bureau of Investigation (F.B.I.) to investigate alleged foreign infiltration of A.I.M. and other activist groups. The B.I.A. was reorganized.

ABOVE Sacheen Littlefeather at the 1973 Academy Awards reading a statement from longtime Hollywood activist Marlon Brando. Winner of the Best Actor Oscar award for his role in the 1972 film *The Godfather II*, Brando had the costumed Littlefeather read a statement denouncing U.S. racism, imperialism, and the poor treatment of Native Americans. Littlefeather, born Maria Cruz, had roles in several 1970s films including *Il Consiliere* and *Johnny Firecloud*.

In 1973, A.I.M. continued its program of activism by seizing and occupying a church at Wounded Knee on the Pine Ridge Indian Reservation. Inspired partially by the 1970 bestseller *Bury My Heart at Wounded Knee*, a recounting of the tragic 1890 massacre on the South Dakota Reservation, the occupiers engaged in a tense standoff with F.B.I. agents. Media attention prevented another bloodbath and the Indians dispersed. But by then the policy championed by President Richard Nixon was beginning to shape federal Indian policy.

The policy, first set in place in 1970, allowed the tribes self-determination without wholesale abandonment by the federal government. It was a fair compromise in lieu of the previous policies which had veered between the extremes for a number of years. As the principles of the new policy were refined, it would lead, though not always smoothly, to the creation of a successful environment of self-determination by the end of the twentieth century.

From this lead, Native Americans began to manage their own affairs at the tribal level, while taking advantage of the federal protection and aid offered to them as a long-suffering, disenfranchised people. In order to maintain this status effectively, the Indians quickly learned how to use statutes and politics to achieve the desired ends. Tribes in Oklahoma began to use their autonomy to establish smoke shops and gambling establishments in opposition to state regulations. The Pequot tribe of Connecticut was the first to succeed with a large-scale gaming operation on reservation land, building the grand Foxwoods Resort-Casino in 1992. An agreement with the state of Connecticut led to the first slot machines in a Native American gaming operation. The income from the casino now provides a number of municipal and social services to the tribe.

While Indian casinos have become so widespread as to shape a new stereotype for Native Americans, their existence and effectiveness must be measured in terms of results. They have to be considered for their effective use of limited reservation land and for income the tribes derive from their operations. Yet not all tribes and individual Native Americans support gambling, still considered by many a vice, as consistent with tribal and cultural values. Government bodies still fight their existence or try to arrange compromises in their size and use. But there is no denying that as the economic muscle behind the right of self-determination, casinos had the largest impact of any development on Native American culture as it entered the new millennium.

CASINOS—BOOM OR BUST?

Tribal Councilor Charlene Jones of the Mashantucket Pequot community agreed to be interviewed for this book and described the history and purpose of the tribe's casino project. Following a series of development projects in the 1970s that did not generate sufficient employment or income, the tribe debated the establishment of gaming on the reservation. In 1986 a high-stakes bingo hall was established, followed by the Foxwoods Casino in 1992. Demand fueled expansion of the facility to a resort with full amenities. An income-sharing agreement with the state of Connecticut allowed slot machines in the casino. The majority of tribal members now appreciate the progress gaming makes possible for them and their neighbors. The resort is a means to an end, not the end in itself.

LEFT The main entrance to the Foxwoods Resort-Casino. The rural Connecticut location of the casino has not been a hindrance to its popularity.

"...this is actually a move, not so much to liberate the island, but to liberate ourselves for the sake of cultural survival..."

Richard Oakes, first Alcatraz occupation spokesperson

ABOVE Foxwoods, the Connecticut resort-casino of the Mashantucket Pequot Tribal Nation, is one of the world's largest casinos.

ABOVE The main entrance to Viejas Casino. The Viejas Band of Mission Indians, along with the Sycuan and Barona Bands, maintain the largest gaming operations in the San Diego area and lead a consortium of Mission bands in driving reservation progress in San Diego County.

Western Shoshone Sacred Land Association

v.1 no.1   April 1980

Land is the Only Issue

We are being asked to sell the future of our people for a mean $1.07 an acre. For thousands of years our people have lived out on this desert. We were able to live a life of happiness because of our intimate knowledge of the gifts of the Creator - the pinenuts, deer and rabbit. We were proud and self-reliant people secure in our land and with our families and communities. Our ancestors passed on to us the way of life that would always insure the continuation of the Shoshone People. Even when confronted with the arrival of Americans, drawn by the discovery of gold in California and silver in Nevada, our ancestors held tightly to their beliefs to be able to pass them down to future generations.

As the number of Americans increased in our territory, our leaders agreed to a treaty of peace and friendship with these new arrivals. The wisdom of our ancestors is also evident in this Treaty of Ruby Valley of 1863. Unlike most treaties with other tribes which gave up large areas of their territories, our treaty confirmed the boundaries of our territory, then called Temoke's Territory after our Chief. In the treaty we allowed the Americans to cross our territory, build railroads, telegraph lines and to establish mining communities, but we did not give up our land. Our leaders were deeply concerned with insuring the Shoshone People would always have a home.

DO WE HAVE THE COURAGE OR WISDOM...TO PROVIDE FOR FUTURE GENERATIONS OF SHOSHONES

Today we are faced with dual crises that once again threaten our land - the land claims payment and the MX missile. We are being asked to sell the rights to our land for $26 million so the Air

cont. on page 8

Land - Yes MX - NO

This declaration is issued to make known to all people of this land the sacred status of the following:

The land is most sacred,
As is the water flowing upon it,
The growing things of the land,
The air we breathe,
The food that grows for us to eat.

All of these things were put here for our use by God and respect is given them by all Indian people of this land. The Western Shoshone people have a duty to protect these things.

In 1863, the United States of America and the Western Shoshone people made the Treaty of Ruby Valley in which the United States acknowledged the boundaries of the Western Shoshone land and, in return, the Western Shoshone agreed to allow the white man to have rights across the land, to mine minerals from the land, and to use the land for towns, farms, and ranches necessary to support the mining. The Western Shoshone have respected that treaty and have allowed the white man to settle within their boundaries.

In 1974, the United States brought a legal action against the Western Shoshone Indians to prohibit their use of their lands. The United States has claimed that all Western Shoshones lands now belong to the United States and is administering them under the Bureau of Land Management and the Forest Service. The United States has been unable to prove this claim under its own laws and has cowardly delayed the lawsuit it started while attempting to acquire the title to these lands by forcing the Western Shoshone to accept fifteen cents an acre for them. Furthermore, the United States has indicated its intention to desecrate these lands by uncontrolled development and implacing massive nuclear weapons.

By these actions, the United States is reneging on its treaty obligations. Therefore, in order to fulfill the sacred obligations of the Western Shoshone people, we give notice to the United states of the following:

1. We declare and mark and describe the boundaries of Western Shoshone lands, once again, as those set forth in the Treaty of Ruby Valley and that the Bureau of Land Management and the Forest Service of the United States are without jurisdiction within those boundaries. The Western Shoshone people understand the need for grazing of livestock by the established operators and do not intend to disturb these operations. The Western Shoshone people also recognize the need to regulate and protect the land, but contend that this must be done lawfully, recognizing the jurisdiction of the Western Shoshone.

2. We declare our opposition to the Desert Land Entry Act which is being abused by outside land speculators. We refuse to recognize the validity of any claim to Western Shoshone land, entry to which was made after May 6, 1974, and will not acknowledge the validity of any further taking of Western Shoshone lands under the Treaty of Ruby Valley

Cartoon by Gunnar Schieder

until such time as the United States of America recognizes its responsibility under the treaty and works out with the Western Shoshone the status of all lands within the treaty boundaries.

3. We declare we are opposed to the State of Nevada establishing a state park at Wild Horse Reservoir and any other state action affecting Western Shoshone lands or waters until such time as the dispute instigated by the United States is resolved and the legal status of Western Shoshone lands and waters is clearly established.

4. We declare we are in opposition to any further exploration, leasing or development or extraction of natural resources and refuse to recognize the validity of any lease or permit issued by the United States after May 6, 1974.

5. We declare that we are opposed to the installation of the MX missile system or any other offensive weapon of war being put on Western Shoshone land.

6. We declare we have the right to hunting, fishing, gathering of all natural Indian foods, herbs and roots, the use of water to make things grow, and the roaming at will of the land as stated in Paragraph 1. In the same respect, we hold all living things, from the largest of animals to the smallest insects to be sacred. And the taking of these is to be done with respect for its life and to be done so sparingly.

7. We declare our right to practice the aboriginal Western Shoshone Indian religion and that we hold all nature to be sacred.

8. We declare that in past history the United States government has not recognized the basic human rights of the Indian people. We declare that we are human and are entitled to all the human rights that are given to us by God, which rights are alluded to in the Constitution of these United States as belonging to all people.

OUR MOTHER EARTH IS SACRED AND IS NOT FOR SALE.

WESTERN SHOSHONE SACRED LAND ASSOCIATION
c/o Raymond Yowell
WAYSACK
Lee, Nevada   89829

NO MX ON SHOSHONE LAND!!

This is Not Air Force Land

By Jerry Mander

BATTLE MOUNTAIN INDIAN COLONY, Nevada—A small tribe of Indians, living in the vastness of the Nevada desert, will soon receive one of the largest "land claim" payments in history. The Indian Claims Commission has awarded the Western Shoshone Indians, as represented by the Temoak Bands, $26,145,189. This money is compensation for 24 million acres of aboriginal Western Shoshone land which was alledgedly "taken" in 1872 by the U.S., following 10,000 years of undisturbed Shoshone occupancy.

The Indians don't want the money. For five years they have tried to stay the claim made in their name. They fired their claims attorney, and they've appealed to the president, the court of claims, and Supreme Court asking each to vacate or stay the claim.

"Nothing happened in 1872, that's just a made-up date," according to Glenn Holley, presently chairman (chief) of the Temoak Bands. "We never lost that land, we never left it, and we're not selling it. In our religion it's forbidden to take money for land. What's really happening is that the government, through this Claims Commission, is stealing the land right now in 1979."

The Shoshones say that the 1863 Treaty of Ruby Valley is still 100 per cent valid. That treaty guarantees U.S. citizens safe passage through Shoshone Territory and allows for some mining and ranching in the desert, while confirming that the boundaries of the Western Shoshone Nation include most of eastern Nevada.

One of the Shoshone's current attorneys, John O'Connell, points out that there has never been any act by the U.S. to extinguish Indian title to the land. "We have asked the government over and over again in court to show evidence of how it obtained title to the Shoshone land. They start groping around and can't find a damn thing. In fact, the relevant documents show that the U.S. never wanted the Nevada desert until just lately. There's not a doubt in my mind that the Western Shoshones still hold legal title to most of their aboriginal territory. The great majority of them still live there and they don't want money for it. They love that desert. But if the Claims Commission is permitted to write its check, the U.S. may have finally stolen the land legally."

All seemed lost a few months ago until Reid Chambers, another of the Shoshone's new attorneys, proposed a last-ditch compromise. He suggested that the Interior Department invoke a clause of the treaty by which the Indians would be given a three million acre reservation, and in turn would "give up their wandering ways." This could be accompanied by some cash settlement. The compromise was received enthusiastically by medium-level government officials. But to everyone's amazement, Secretary of the Interior Cecil Andrus broke off all negotiations in June without a counter offer. His only comment was, "It would not be in the best interest of the Indians."

Two weeks later, President Carter announced that the first choice for deployment of the $33 billion MX missile, an integral part of the Salt II proposal, was the "public land" in the Nevada desert, "currently under the Bureau of Land Management." Virtually all of this "public land" falls within the boundaries of Western Shoshones territory.

'Land, Not Money'

That a small number of Indians would refuse $26 million for mostly arid desert may seem crazy, particularly since the average family income among the Shoshones is only $3000 a year. "The grass is so sparse there," one Interior official said, "the cows have to graze at 40 mph just to get enough to eat."

My own experience of the Nevada desert was typical of most people's, as an occasional driver on Interstate 80, where all I could see was hour after hour of dull, brown wasteland. A few months ago, however, I hiked off the highway into that desert world of juniper and sagebrush flats and strange, bare folded mountains. The light is alive there like no place in this country save parts of the New Mexico desert. The moods and colors change dramatically from hour to hour and soon, the land itself begins to dominate urbanite preconceptions. "All of this land, everything in it, is medicine," one old Shoshone woman told me.

The nuances of the desert are not obscure to the Shoshones. They have been sustained by this "wasteland" for more than 100 generations, roaming through it in small bands, all the way from central Utah to southern California. Hidden in the valleys and on certain ridgetops are large pine-nut (pinyon) forests that have provided the staple food, as well as forest cover for deer and small animals which together formed the Indians' subsistence.

With the intrusion of whites only four generations ago, all of this started to change. But the major recent development came less than a decade ago. The Bureau of Land Management took it upon itself to destroy more than one million acres of these pine-nut groves. They killed the trees in the most terrifying manner, pulling them down with gigantic iron chains dragged between BLM bulldozers. After clearing the pinyons, the BLM has planted grass in hopes of attracting white ranchers.

The destruction of the Shoshones' subsistence base, and with it the undermining of their traditional cohesion, has put them in the position of having to seek support from white society. While some of the Indians have been able to maintain their self-sufficiency, many of the Shoshones have moved into settlements, appropriately called "colonies," adjoining white communities. The men seek jobs working as miners or on ranches when such work is available. The women hire out as domestics or waitresses. Though unemployment figures are slightly misleading when applied to a culture which still partially sustains itself off the land, the U.S. government puts the average unemployment figure at 30 to 50 per cent depending upon the community. Many are on welfare. Glenn Holley himself, unpaid as chief of the Temoak Bands, is a former copper miner now partially living on disability payments caused by a mine injury.

Despite this "poverty," the Indians maintain their staunch refusal to accept any cash payment for the desert land which they say is legally theirs and which provides them their cultural, economic, and spiritual identity.

Lawyers and Money

In 1945, the Indian Claims Act was considered a liberal reform. At last a mechanism existed "to settle finally any and all legal, equitable and moral obligations that the United States might owe to the Indians." But there were some wrinkles in it.

The law did not permit the resolution of grievances by any means other than cash payment for lost lands. Rather than being able to seek help enforcing treaty rights or to stop the cutting down of trees, Indians could ask for money by asserting they'd lost their land. If so, the land title was permanently lost and the Indians were barred from seeking any other redress.

Secondly, any tribal member could sue in behalf of the whole tribe. This claimant's attorney then became the sole representative of the tribe. The net effect was to preclude participation of any Indians with other points of view.

Probably the worst element of the law gave claims attorneys commissions of up to 10 per cent of the total award, thus producing a new breed of attorney, getting wealthy by seeking-out Indians willing to file claims. It also gave the lawyers every incentive they needed to urge Indian governments to convert their diverse grievances into cash claims. Eventually, the Indians noticed they were in effect *selling* land for which they might still prove valid title.

The western Shoshones had a clear grievance. Since 1910 they'd been asking the U.S. to stop calling the Shoshone treaty land "public domain." Their protests were ignored. By the 1930s, the Shoshones had two legal advisers, one of whom was Ernest Wilkinson, a partner in the Washington law firm of Wilkinson, Cragun and Barker. According to John O'Connell, Wilkinson suggested that the Indians join him in lobbying a new law through Congress by which Indians could obtain cash settlements for lost land. The Shoshones refused, saying that they had not lost their lands and only wanted to confirm that fact.

At some point after the Indians Claims Act was passed, Wilkinson introduced the Shoshones to his partner, Robert W. Barker, who advised the Indians that the only viable course was to seek a cash claim. A group of Shoshones, including the Temoak Bands tribal council as then constituted, agreed to let him proceed.

Barker filed the claim in 1951, asserting that the Western Shoshones had lost not only their treaty lands, but also their aboriginal land extending into Death Valley, California. He included in the 24 million acre claim some 16 million acres that the Shoshones say were never occupied by anyone but Indian bands, and which were never lost. But the U.S. Justice Department *agreed* with Barker's contention, and, as a result, the Claims Commission did not investigate or seek arguments to the contrary. They awarded the Shoshones $26 million, based on an average land value in 1872 of $1.05 per acre, plus some unpaid mineral royalties. (An average acre of Nevada desert now brings about $200.)

When this claim is paid, Wilkinson, Cragen and Barker expect to receive about $2.5 million.

"We should have listened to our old people," said Raymond Yowell, a member of the Temoak tribal council and a one-time supporter of the claim. "They'd been telling us that Barker was selling out our lands. It took me years to realize it. It's very complicated. But the deeper you dig the more obvious it becomes."

In an article in the *Native Nevadan*, Yowell attempted to show how Barker had engineered a kind of paper support from a tribe that was basically opposed to what he was doing. At a 1965 mass meeting called to get tribal approval of a loan needed to pursue the claims: "a majority of the people present objected to the way Barker was giving up the remaining rights to our lands and walked out . . . soon after at an Elko meeting about 80 per cent of the people showed their opposition by walking out. It is important that at these meetings Barker insisted that we had no choice as to whether to keep title to some lands or give them up for the claims money. The only choice was to either approve or disapprove the loan. And if we disapproved we would get nothing. After the majority left, those Indians remaining, about 25 or 30, elected me and Jackie Woods members of the Claims Committee," which approved Barker's loan. (Tragically, traditional Indian people tend to express disapproval by boycotting meetings, walking out, and refusing to vote. This is logical among Indians themselves, but when dealing with whites the effect has been to leave the deal making to the Indians who are into deal-making.)

In 1974, Glen Holley and others formed the Western Shoshone Legal Defense and Education Association which hired John O'Connell as attorney and filed a petition to intervene with the Claims Commission, charging Barker with collusion with the government. Barker says now that the collusion charge was merely a technical point to allow the Shoshones to argue their case.

"Most of our people never understood that by filing with the Claims Commission we'd be agreeing that we lost our land," said Holley." They thought we were just clarifying the title question. Barker kept saying the claim was for land we had already lost . . . that we weren't selling anything. We wanted to show we hadn't lost the land."

Despite these sentiments Barker fought the association's petition.

When they lost the petition, O'Connell appealed to the Court of Claims. Barker fought the apeal. The court agreed with Barker that the Temoak bands had *chosen* a long time before to give up the land for money and that it was "too late to upset the apple cart after the fruit has been so carefully collected and piled."

By 1976, the Temoak band had gone through a complete revolution and voted to seek a stay of the claim until the land question could be considered. Barker fought them again. The court denied the stay.

Finally, the Temoak band fired Barker. He also fought the firing and is still fighting to be recognized as attorney of record, though in any event he stands to reap the benefits of his 30 years of advice and council to the Indians.

In 1977, a new attorney, Reid Chambers, was hired and he proposed the three million acre compromise mentioned earlier. But despite enthusiasm by many government people, Andrus mysteriously rejected the compromise. Though he did not expect it to succeed, Chambers filed an appeal with the Supreme Court arguing that the Shoshone have been prevented at every stage from presenting their case on land title. Now they stand to lose everything "without ever having a had a day in court," said Chamber's appeal. Last week, like every court before it, the Supreme Court refused to hear arguments in the case. The lawyers for the Shoshones are now contemplating what other legal moves are possible, but at this moment only one other case has any potential to slow things down.

Dann Sisters' Case

Mary and Carrie Dann are two Shoshone sisters who live with their brother and Carrie's children on a ranch outside of Crescent Valley, Nevada. In 1974, the Dann sisters were herding cattle near home when a Bureau of Land Management ranger stopped them and demanded to see their grazing permit. The Danns replied that they didn't need a permit since this wasn't U.S. land, but Shoshone Nation. They were charged with trespass.

"I have grazed my cattle and horses on that land all of my life," Carrie Dann told me, "and my mother did before me and her mother before her. Our people have been on this land for thousands of years. We don't need a permit to graze here."

The trespass case went to the U.S. district court in Reno. The Dann sisters convinced attorney John O'Connell, ordinarily a criminal attorney, to invoke a treaty-rights argument. O'Connell asked the court for a summary judgment based on the Danns' aboriginal rights, and challenged the Justice Department to show a shred of evidence demonstrating how and when the U.S. had obtained title. The U.S. couldn't produce. Instead, in a typical Catch-22, it referred the court to the Claims Commission case which found that the land had been taken in 1872. But in reality, the Claims Commission had not "found" anything of the sort. It had merely accepted Robert Barker's assertion of title extinguishment. Still, this was enough for the Reno judge who ruled against the Danns, fined them $500, and ordered them off the land.

O'Connell appealed to the Ninth Circuit Court of Appeals, repeating that there was no evidence anywhere, including in the ICC case, that the Indians had lost title. In a tremendous victory for the Western Shoshones, the appeals court agreed with the Danns and remanded the case to the lower court for trial on the land title question.

The date of this appeals court reversal was March 15, 1978.

In the intervening year and a half, the Danns have repeatedly tried to bring their case to trial but have been met with delays by the court. "The judge has been stalling," said O'Connell. "He never wanted that trial. At one point I accused the government of deliberately delaying the Dann case long enough to get the Indian claims check written under the theory that once the payment was received, Indian title would have been extinguished and the Danns would have been prevented from asserting it. The judge admitted on the record that he was 'sympathetic with the government's strategy.'"

The MX Missile

October 7. A meeting is called by Glenn Holley and Raymond Yowell to discuss a bizarre new development. The government plans to put the MX missile on Shoshone aboriginal land. About 100 representatives of Shoshone communities around the state are in attendance. Also present are representatives of several environmental and disarmament groups, including SANE and Clergy and Laity Concerned.

Holley and Yowell explain in intermittent Shoshone and English that the MX is

→

Mother Earth is not for sale

Testimony of Raymond Yowell, Chairman of the Western Shoshone Sacred Land Association before the House Interior Subcommittee on Public Lands

Mr. Chairman: My name is Raymond Yowell and I am Chairman of the Western Shoshone Sacred Land Association which is an organization of traditional Western Shoshone Indians dedicated to preserving the Western Shoshone ancestral lands, culture and religion.

I am also former chairman of the Temoak Bands of Western Shoshone, the federally recognized tribe to which I belong, and a former chairman of the Nevada Inter-Tribal Council which is the umbrella organization for all organized Indian groups in Nevada.

Both the Inter-Tribal Council and the Western Shoshone Sacred Land Association have unanimously passed resolutions opposing the placing of the MX in Nevada.

Many of the reasons for our opposition are the same as those you have heard and will hear today from others, but the main concern of the Western Shoshone is unique - a large portion of the lands coveted by the Air Force for this project is Western Shoshone land.

"...THESE LANDS ARE NOT IN THE PUBLIC DOMAIN AND NEVER HAVE BEEN"

Therefore, Mr. Chairman, I give you a very simple reason why these lands cannot be withdrawn from the public domain, and that is that these lands are not in the public domain and never have been.

Congress in the 1860's not only failed to extinguish the Western Shoshone title, it specifically and explicitly decided to not extinguish Western Shoshone title. Instead, it sent treaty commissioners to negotiate the Treaty of Ruby Valley which gave the whiteman all he wanted -- rights of way through the lands and the right to mine and homestead, but left the vacant lands to the Western Shoshone -- some 15.8 million acres.

This came as rather a shock to the government when we raised it in a trespass suit brought by the government against some Western Shoshone Indians in 1974, but the staff lawyers in the Interior Department know it is true, and the District Court in Reno knows it is true. They have frantically stalled that trespass suit for six years now. Last spring the Interior Department formed a task force to negotiate a compromise, but that was squelched by the Secretary of Interior -- about the same time as Nevada was selected as a site for the MX missile.

The Executive Branch has a plan to get around the embarrassing fact that the Western Shoshone have title to these lands. Over the objection of the Western Shoshone, they pushed a claim through the Indian Claims Commission to compensate us for the lands, based upon the fiction that the lands were taken in 1872 when they were worth 15¢ an acre.

IT DOES NOT STOP US FROM SUEING THIRD PARTIES, SUCH AS CONTRACTORS TRYING TO BUILD A MISSILE SYSTEM

This plan will not work. First, that is a fraudulent judgement. Second, the Court of Appeals for the Ninth Circuit has already held that judgement does not stop us from asserting title because it was the result of a stipulation rather than a judgement. Third, even if it were a valid binding judgement, all that payment does is bar the Indians from bringing another claim against the U.S. It does not change the title and it does not stop us from sueing third parties, such as contractors, trying to build a missile system.

WE WILL NOT BE MOVED.
WE WILL NOT BE BOUGHT OFF.
OUR MOTHER EARTH IS NOT FOR SALE

Mr. Chairman, these lands are sacred to my people -- they were given to us long before Moses brought the people of Israel out of Egypt. Archeologists tell us that we are the oldest continuous culture in one spot known to modern man.

We will not be moved.
We will not be bought off.
Our Mother Earth is not for sale.
Thank you for listening.

The Western Shoshone settlement award is $26 million, compensation for 27 million acres or approximately $1.05 an acre. However, the 15.8 million acres the Western Shoshone still own and are fighting the U.S. for recognition of that ownership, was considered "poor grazing land" and hence valued at only 15¢ an acre.

In early March, the Western Shoshone took their case before an international forum, the United Nations Human Rights Commission in Geneva, Switzerland.

The member nations represented on the Commission responded to the testimony with active questioning and interest. All nations represented except one, expressed their support for the Western Shoshone case and acknowledged the importance of the international forum.

In light of President Carter's emphasis on championing human rights issues, maybe this will remind him that, regarding the Western Shoshone land claim, the whole world is watching.

---

the largest construction project in U.S. history and that it will bring some 20,000 new people onto their land. Ten thousand miles of road are planned in the desert, equal to one-fourth of the U.S. interstate highway system. Construction will require 3.15 billion gallons of water, endangering an already overused water table. Two hundred nuclear warheads would be moving around on trucks through the desert. The whole area "will act as a kind of giant sponge of targets in the U.S.," said Holley. "To absorb the Russian nuclear attack. Probably the U.S. figures that's okay since there's nobody out here but us Indians."

A resolution against the MX is passed unanimously. The statement expresses anger with the government for "assuming the land belongs to the U.S.," and it blames the MX for Andrus's cutoff of negotiations. "It's ironic that the U.S. is violating a treaty with one nation to secure passage of a treaty with another," said John Redhouse.

After the meeting I approached O'Connell to ask if he thought someone might have laid an arm on Andrus, because of the MX.

"I doubted it at first," he said, "but I don't know. Andrus acted awfully suddenly and against a lot of advice."

I decided to ask around about this possibility and called Major Art Forester at the Air Force Information Office. "Yes, the Air Force does know about the land dispute with the Indians, but no, there've been no attempts to talk with either Justice or Interior about it."

I then called or visited four different bureaucrats at Interior, and three at Justice, all of whom had been involved at various stages with the Shoshone case. None of them had heard the MX mentioned, though one, who asked not to be named, called it "extremely plausible" that Andrus was contacted, "probably by the National Security Council."

When I tried to reach Andrus himself, his assistant informed me that the secretary was not involved in the case and doesn't know much about it." So who wrote that letter Andrus signed? "Leo Krulitz."

Krulitz is the Interior Department's chief lawyer and its second most powerful man. He had been described to me in several quarters as totally devoted to "clarifying" all Indian title issues in favor of the U.S. By now it was clear that he had made the decision on the Shoshone case and he'd done it mostly alone.

I was able to reach Krulitz on the phone and asked why the negotiations for a reservation had been cut off.

"Well, I wasn't that comfortable with Reid Chambers's claim that the Indians still seem to possess title, but really didn't give the legal issues much thought They were so complex that I addressed it as a policy question.

I asked him what a "policy question" was.

"Well, under no circumstances was I going to recommend that we create a reservation without first going to Congress. But the Indians can always do that themselves."

I reminded him that the Treaty of Ruby Valley gives Interior clear authority to establish a reservation and, practically speaking, since the Nevada delegation is one of the more conservative in the country, the Indians had no real chance to go that route.

"I saw my job," he said, "as assessing the resource needs of the Shoshones, but I couldn't recommend that we establish a reservation."

I asked him what he meant by "in the best interests of the Indians," when he refused their compromise.

"What I meant is that this money is sitting there in the Claims Commission and it's a lot of money, you know You have to realize these are very poor, very destitute people, living in disparate communities. I just thought they ought to have the money.

What about the MX missile? "No, that came along much later."

In fact, the Andrus letter had preceded the MX announcement by only a few weeks, but by this time I had lost interest in the fine points of secret MX dealings, I realize the MX is only different by degree from the prior destruction of the pine forests and that both are just symptomatic of the larger crime the Shoshones have been trying to broadcast since 1910. The U.S. is stealing the Shoshone land. The bureaucrats involved are not really concerned about the legalities or the matter of what the Indians have to say about it. They are just following a set of rules, a logic of procedure, begun a long time ago, which obscures to the world, even to themselves, the knowledge of what they're actually doing. By now, it just seems right to clean up the loose ends.

Finally, I asked Krulitz if he had any personal feelings about the injustice being visited upon the Shoshones. He seemed shocked at the question.

"Certainly there's been no injustice from anyone in the Interior Department," he said. ∎

I TELL YA, JIMBO... WE GOTTA WATCH THEM RUSSKIES LIKE A HAWK. THEY'LL BREAK A TREATY QUICKER THAN YOU CAN BLINK AN EYE...

YOU TELL 'IM, FORKED TONGUE

Condensed from December 17, 1979, Village Voice article by Jerry Mander

cont. from page 1

OUR ANCESTORS PASSED ON TO US THE WAY OF LIFE THAT WOULD ALWAYS INSURE THE CONTINUATION OF THE SHOSHONE PEOPLE

Force can build the largest weapon system ever designed. Are we willing to sell? Do we have the courage or wisdom of our ancestors to provide for the future generations of Shoshones? One hundred years from now, if there are any Shoshones left, how will they look at our generation as ancestors? Will they speak with pride about the struggle of their ancestors to preserve the land for future generations or will they talk of our generation with shame as the one that sold out? How will our own children view us when they become adults and have no land on which to raise their families? Will their memories of the land claims struggle be simply a few good drunks, some new clothes, a fancy car? Are we thinking of the future or only the present?

'All around us the signs of economic collapse are growing. Inflation continues out of control. Private investors are putting their money into gold and real estate to protect their capital in event of such a collapse. Anyone who remembers the depression knows that those with land were at least able to feed their families while those in the cities went hungry. While anyone with money is investing in real estate, we are selling our land for $1.07 an acre. The land, our Mother Earth, will continue to take care of us as long as we do not abuse her and continue to return thanks to her. She has continued to do that for thousands of years. Now some of us want to sell her so the Air Force can rip her heart out and make her a destroyer rather than a giver of life.

SOME OF US WANT TO SELL MOTHER EARTH SO THE AIR FORCE CAN RIP HER HEART OUT AND MAKE HER A DESTROYER RATHER THAN A GIVER OF LIFE

Now those people want to put this giant missile system, the MX, in our territory. It will destroy many of our sacred burial sites, destroy plant and animal life, bring thousands of newcomers, use up our precious water, and change our whole way of life. Our ranching and farming neighbors, for the first time, are beginning to understand what it means to be an Indian. They, too, see their way of life threatened by the military and the federal government. For once, perhaps, we can put aside our past differences and join hands with our non-Indian neighbors to fight this menace to our land.

We can say no to MX and no to the land claims. They cannot build the missile as long as we own the land. Our Sioux brothers and sisters are currently saying no to a $103 million claim for the Black Hills because of their sacred importance. They have also joined together with non-Indian ranchers to try to prevent uranium mining in the Black hills that threatens

their way of life. The Indian people of Santo Domingo Pueblo in New Mexico have also recently fired their land claims attorney and intend to fight for their lands. In California, the land claims payment took years to distribute. Here the government is attempting to force the payment on us as quickly as possible so we don't hang up their MX missile plans.

THE MONEY IS ONLY TEMPORARY, LAND IS FOREVER

We need to look closely at what we are giving up and its effect on coming generations of Shoshone. The money is only temporary, land is forever. If we have any concern for children and grandchildren, we should fight for the land. We ask you to join us in making land the only issue.

RESOLUTION OF THE GREAT BASIN MX ALLIANCE

Great Basin MX Alliance

WHEREAS, the MX Missile System is planned for the Great Basin area of the western United States;
WHEREAS, this project would jeopardize the lives, liberty and property of all our citizens, in that it is intended to draw as a sponge the missiles of any hostile nation;
WHEREAS, the impact of building this vast, questionable defense system would place an enormous strain on the already unstable state of the nation's economy;
WHEREAS, it is well recognized that this huge expenditure of Federal money can only tremendously aggravate the runaway inflation of the U.S.;
WHEREAS, the social and cultural structure of this central western area would be irrevocably changed by an exploding population;
WHEREAS, the natural resources of the area would be consumed by this single, non-productive use, which would preclude the normal, constructive develop-

ment of these resources that is essential to our nation's welfare;
WHEREAS, the long established economy of the Great Basin region is based upon farming, ranching and mining, in the production of food, fiber and minerals;
WHEREAS, the acquisition, exploitation or destruction by the Federal government of the aforesaid lands and resources will directly affect the ability of these industries to produce, or even to survive;
WHEREAS, encompassed within the Great Basin are several Native American tribes; and the executive, legislative and judicial branches of the Federal government are legally and morally bound to uphold Native American rights;
WHEREAS, the Air Force has not made sufficient guarantees that the Native American land water and treaty rights, religious freedom, archeological resources and burial grounds would be preserved,

protected and upheld as prescribed by treaties and Acts of Congress, and judicial review;
WHEREAS, the water necessary for the construction and maintenance of the proposed missile project is to be drawn from a very finite and already overburdened Great Basin aquifier;
WHEREAS, the vegetative cover of the region is spare, fragile, often miniature in size, and unable to withstand any but the most modest impact;
WHEREAS, the wildlife of the region are directly dependent upon a fragile desert environment, and require a vast unbroken habitat for their existence;
WHEREAS, no suitable plan has been set forth for the perpetuation and protection of these unique animal species;
WHEREAS, the Air Force has been less than candid about the kinds and degrees of impact on people and resources in the proposed deployment

area, and it is manifestly impossible to prepare an adequate Environmental Impact Statement within the Air Force time frame;
WHEREAS, military experts have identified the proposed MX Missile System as having questionable defense value;
WHEREAS, more cost-effective military alternatives have not been adequately considered;
NOW THEREFORE BE IT RESOLVED, the Great Basin MX Alliance urged the elected officials of the states of Nevada and Utah, and the officials of all the other states whose future welfare must be considered, to oppose the present Air Force plans for the deployment of the MX missile in the Great Basin.

This resolution was adopted by the Great Basin MX Alliance on March 1, 1980. The alliance is comprised of ranchers, miners, farmers, businessmen, Native Americans, sportsmen, recreationists, and conservationists from the states of Nevada, Utah, and Wyoming.

What People Can Do ...

*Donations are urgently needed. We face rapidly mounting litigation costs in our land claims struggle. Expenses incurred traveling to and from public hearings and other speaking engagements to publicize our plight against the MX are also rapidly mounting. Donations will assist us in carrying on this fight.
*Other resources people would be willing to share will also be appreciated.
*If you belong to an organization interested in our cause, invite our speakers to address your organization. We have the film "Broken Treaty

at Battle Mountain" that we can show. We are also in the process of developing a multi media presentation on the Western Shoshone land struggle to take up where the film leaves off and bring people up to date. We are willing to travel to these meetings but require financial assistance to help meet the travel expenses.
*If you hear of meetings or public hearings that are important to attend, please let us know. We will try to send someone.
*Help us bolster legislative support. Write letters to

your Senators and Representatives in Congress, especially those on key committees deciding the fate of the MX.
*Inform your community through "Letters to the Editor" in your local newspaper.
*Press elected officials, local, state and federal, to take a stand against the MX and supporting the Western Shoshone.
*If you live in a possible deployment area, organize your community or join forces with others to campaign against the missile.

Donations are tax deductible.
Make checks payable to Western Shoshone Sacred Land Association/The Youth Project.

For more info, contact:
Western Shoshone Sacred
    Land Association
c/o Raymond Yowell
WAYSACK
Lee, Nevada 89829

For more info on the MX, contact:
SANE
514 C Street, N.E.
Washington D.C. 20002
(202) 546-4868

RETURN TO THE PAST: ANCIENT INFLUENCES & MODERN LIFE

NATIVE AMERICANS—AS THIS WORK HAS ATTEMPTED TO POINT OUT—
ARE SPIRITUAL PEOPLE, IN TOUCH WITH NATURE, IN TOUCH WITH THE
PAST, IN TOUCH, PERHAPS, WITH THE SPIRITS OF ALL THINGS PAST,
PRESENT, AND FUTURE. A NEW MILLENNIUM HAS JUST BEGUN.

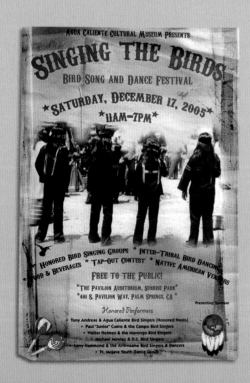

ABOVE Today many tribal cultural centers sponsor or co-sponsor outreach programs to involve Native Americans and the general public in different aspects of tribal culture. This poster is for a music and dance festival by the Agua Caliente band of Mission Indians, an enriching opportunity that also includes the art of bird singing.

While this concept of time expressed in years and centuries is more important to historians than it is to traditional Native American values, the people are still affected by the march of time and the technology and pace of life that accompanies that march. Many Native Americans have assimilated the broader culture outside their own. Whether they live on reservations among their own people or in houses and apartments in cities and suburbs, they embrace many aspects of modern society. But keeping up with the world of commerce, education, entertainment, and advancement does not mean they drift away from their culture and their past. Pow-wows, harvest festivals, and educational and cultural exchanges are popular forms of interchange and enjoyment for many Native Americans. And, when welcomed in, they have a positive impact on people of other cultures as well.

It is understandable that some events Native Americans celebrate together must be done in private or among small groups; hence photography and recording are sometimes restricted. But that doesn't restrict a pow-wow, rodeo, or harvest festival to only those directly involved. Others can observe these experiences and enjoy and learn. Pow-wows are probably the oldest and most popular forum for Native Americans to meet and exchange ideas and goods. When tribes began to lose

PRESERVING NATIVE AMERICAN HERITAGE

Native American culture is experiencing a period of unprecedented growth. The recent establishment of the Smithsonian National Museum of the American Indian marks a new visibility to the study and exhibition of the culture. Throughout the United States and Canada, many other new museums, cultural centers, and historic sites are being established. Nearly all major universities and colleges have programs of Native American studies. Seminars and other opportunities to bring Native Americans and non-natives together for mutual understanding are on the rise. Because this growth is dynamic, an archive of new information will continue beyond this work. Information on how to learn and get involved is at the back of this book on page 160.

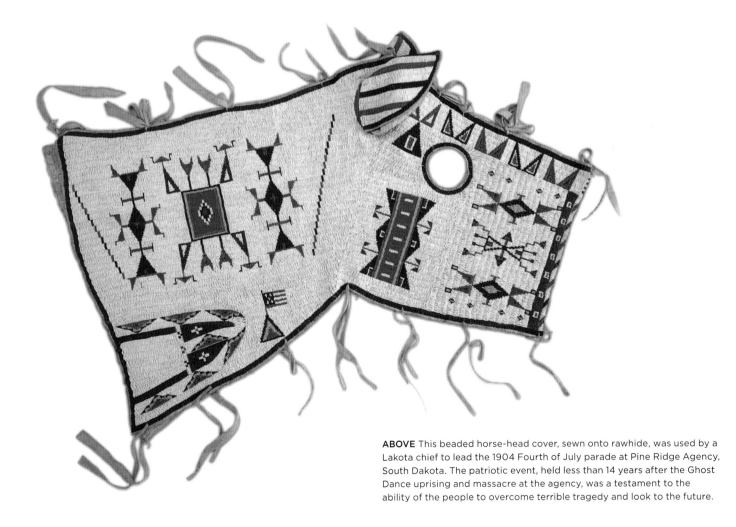

ABOVE This beaded horse-head cover, sewn onto rawhide, was used by a Lakota chief to lead the 1904 Fourth of July parade at Pine Ridge Agency, South Dakota. The patriotic event, held less than 14 years after the Ghost Dance uprising and massacre at the agency, was a testament to the ability of the people to overcome terrible tragedy and look to the future.

ABOVE These Native Americans dressed in the regalia of Great Plains warriors ride in a staged re-enactment. Re-enactments of Indian Wars battles began on stage in the theatrical Wild West shows of Buffalo Bill and others, then were brought outdoors to commemorate famous battles and entertain tourists.

members to the cities and other off-reservation pursuits in the early twentieth century, the pow-wows brought them back together. And the events grew and expanded to become, in some cases, intertribal events.

Among the many responsibilities of tribal councils today is ensuring that their relations with their community are sound. Many reach out to foster understanding and tolerance in a variety of ways. Museums and cultural centers have been created from tribal resources in an effort to involve the public in understanding the complex culture and history of the tribe and of Native Americans as a people. Others have initiated visiting artist, dance, and educational programs, as well as sponsoring their own promising artists and scholars to achieve a broader understanding through grants and foundations.

Finally, the public institutions, foundations, and interested individuals of the United States and Canada, recognizing the importance of the culture of their original inhabitants, have made commitments to broadening the understanding of Native Americans. Many state and local museums, historic sites, and periodic events focus on Native Americans. National museums and institutions foster study and involvement in the cultures of the various tribes and Native Americans in general, as an important segment of the population, whose people are to be commended for their patience, admired for their courage, and embraced for their unique contributions to the world, now and in times past and future.

ABOVE TOP Native American weavers at the Hubbell Trading Post National Historic Site on the Navajo Nation in northeast Arizona engage in the art of traditional blanket making on a vertical loom to the delight and amazement of visitors to the park.

ABOVE MIDDLE Two Native American women enjoy the 8th Annual Intertribal Pow-wow—Journey Home—at the Frisco Native American Museum, Frisco, North Carolina, held in April 2006. Chery (left) is a member of an Eastern tribe. Lori can trace her heritage to the Hatteras tribe of Hatteras Island where the annual event takes place.

ABOVE BOTTOM This reconstructed Chumash village is at the Thousand Oaks Chumash Cultural Center in Southern California. Shown here are three 'aps (thatched roof huts) made with willow-branch frames and woven tule-reed coverings, which were family dwellings. The village also includes two temescals (sweat lodges), a granary, bonfire pit, and a recreated burial ground.

POW-WOWS

Pow-wows, both tribal and intertribal, give families, tribal members, and even those distantly connected the opportunity to meet or reunite and exchange news and ideas first hand. In most cases, dance and craft demonstrations, food, and object displays are open to all. Museum founder Carl Bornfriend (Lenape), of the Frisco Native American Museum in Hatteras, North Carolina, is very proud of the long-running annual pow-wow there. "Our Pow-wow, 'Journey Home,' is the result of one of humankind's longest-running needs and traditions. We are most gratified to celebrate on ancient ancestral ground where ALL are welcome in peace, love, and appreciation."

ABOVE A Havasupai rodeo staged in northwestern Arizona in 1947. A popular and lasting tradition of Native American cultures of the west is the rodeo. It combines the horsemanship that has been part of the culture for more than 300 years, the competitive spirit that has existed even longer as part of coming of age and leadership traditions, and the cowboy skills learned as these Indians adapted to ranching.

PAGE 18: QUEENS CITY DEED

This Instrument of writing witnesseth unto all Christian people to whom it may come or any ways concern, know ye, that whereas I [the] underwritten Munagoab, an Indian and chief sachem of all lands commonly called and known by the name of Rockaway situated to the southwest of the town of Homestead, within Queen's County upon Long Island and within the precincts thereof, do by these presents and for and upon divers considerations and former favours, received from Thomas Townsend of Oyster Bay within the said county abovesaid, have freely given as a free gift without any reservation, unto the abovesaid Thomas Townsend, one neck of land being and adjoining to Homestead mill on the west side of the said mill from the first bound northwest, whereof beginneth at the head of the swamp called in the Indian language Cuppone, and from thence upon a straight line eastwardly to the northward most part of the said mill dam and from thence by the said mill from southwardly to the meadow and thence westwardly by the said meadow to the river or swamp called as abovesaid Cuppone and from thence northwardly to the head of the said swamp first bounder, including within the said bounds or neck of land as above bounded [63acres] It in quantity more or less for and upon the reasons and consideration as abovesaid I have freely and absolutely given unto the abovesaid Thomas Townsend, his heirs, executors administrators or assignees for ever, to have and to hold occupy possess and enjoy without let hindrance or molestation, as his or their own proper right title interest from me or any from by or under me for ever, or any after claims, to the promises by either Christian or Indians laying claim thereto by virtue of any former grant sale or gift I do hereby oblige my self heirs and successors to uphold maintain and make the said neck or tract of land as above bounded good to the said Thomas Townsend his heirs and successors or assignees if molested in the possession or improvement thereof as firmly to all intents constructions or purposes as might be written or worded. According to law to the confirmation of this my deed of gift I have set to my hand and seal. In Oyster Baye this first day of January 1684 the word meadow being interlined before the signing hereof, this above written signed sealed and delivered

IN presence of us
ADAM Wright
GODION Wright
ISAAK Daughey
RICHARD R Corby
CHOPY sachem of Masopag his mark
SUSCANDMEN his mark
JOB Wright
JOHN R Rogers his mark
MUNGOAB his mark & seal
I [the] underwritten Pamun brother to Mungoab sachem do acknowledge his abovesaid gift to Thomas Townsend, as witness my hand and seal
PAMUN his mark and seal

PAGE 62: EMANCIPATION PROCLAMATION

The Supreme Federal Government, has deigned to empower me with its order dated 17th May 1832, endorsing the safety measures set out in the instructions which were previously forwarded to the two Political Heads who preceded me to emancipate the newly converted old Christians of the Missions of this country who are of good character: to share out among them land and some property to encourage their development: to adopt measures for their particular style of government similar to the system prevailing in the Republic; so that, by rescuing from the wretched state in which they find themselves, and getting them to like work, they

might acquire property, make progress and improve their lot. Taking into account their current situation, the enforcement of the orders of the Supreme Court, the laws of 9th November 1812, 4th January and 13th September 1813, the preservation of Missions in order to disseminate the Catholic faith: (23a) I have agreed that property is distributed to government: promotion of agriculture (23a) subject to approval of the Mayor and Holy Mothers, I have agreed to enclosures, farmyards and cattle pens; to build the town halls, Churches, and prisons and any other buildings that they may need: they will cover the dividing lines of the boundaries of the plots (?) of land with fruit trees and other useful trees which may be used as xxx and xxx.

22a Land which is vacant due to death of the owner and his heirs returns to State ownership.

23a Emancipated slaves who neglect their duties and flocks, or who drive them away or do not cultivate their land or abandon their homes to wander and abandon themselves to idleness and vice, will be taken back to the Mission from where they came after assessment by the Mayor and parish priest, who, before acting against those who are at fault will ask them twice to mend their ways and give them sufficient time to improve their behavior.

24a The authorities will ensure that the safety measures are carried out and will be responsible for infringements if they judge that they cannot be remedied.

San Diego, 15 July 1883

PAGE 69: RUSSIAN ALEUT PRIMER

Names of Months in Old Russian	Names of Months in their Order	The letters of the old Russian alphabet	Names of the letters in old Russian (phonetic pronunciations)	Cardinal numbers	Ordinal numbers
January	January	a		1	I
February	February	v		2	II
March	March	g		3	III
April	April	d		4	IV
May	May	f		5	V
June	June	e		6	VI
July	July	s		7	VII
August	August	z		8	VIII
September	September	n		9	IX
October	October	dh		10	X
November	November	i		11	XI
December	December	ai			

Note:
On the top of the title there is written the same thing but in the old Russian. On the left side of the names of the months, the priest has written them again, but this time using the old Russian.

INDEX

(Page numbers in *italics* refer to pictures, photographs and captions, ***italic bold*** to maps)

A SAMPLE OF WEBSITES RELEVANT TO NATIVE AMERICAN STUDY:

www.nmai.si.edu, www.cherokee.org, www.hopi.org,
www.iroquois.net, www.seminoletribe.com,
www.nativeamericanmuseum.org, www.chumashcenter.org,
www.morongonation.org, www.autrynationalcenter.org,
www.okhistory.org, www.nps.gov, www.pequotmuseum.org,
www.oneida-nation.net, www.spokanetribe.com

SELECTED BIBLIOGRAPHY

Bailey, Garrick and Roberta Glenn: *A History of the Navajos: The
    Reservation Years* (Santa Fe, NM: School of American Research
    Press, 1999)
Bolt, Christine: *American Indian Policy and American Reform: Case
    Studies of the Campaign to Assimilate the American Indians*
    (London; Boston: Allen & Unwin, 1987)
Fortunate Eagle, Adam; photo essays by Ilka Hartmann: *Alcatraz!
    Alcatraz!: The Indian Occupation of 1969–1971* (Berkeley: Heyday
    Books, 1992)
Herb, Angela M.: *Beyond the Mississippi: Early Westward Expansion of
    the United States* (New York: Lodestar
    Books, 1996)
Meredith, Howard: *A Short History of the Native Americans in the
    United States* (Malabar, FL: Krieger Publishing Company, 2001)
Michno, Gregory F.: *Encyclopedia of Indian Wars: Western Battles and
    Skirmishes, 1850–1890* (Missoula, MT: Mountain Press Pub. Co., 2003)
Missall, John and Mary Lou: *The Seminole Wars: America's Longest
    Indian Conflict* (Gainesville: University Press of Florida, 2004)
Moore, Jr., Robert J.: *Native Americans: A Portrait: The Art and
    Travels of Charles Bird King, George Catlin, and Karl Bodmer* (New
    York: Stewart, Tabori & Chang, 1997)
Nester, William R.: *The Great Frontier War: Britain, France, and the
    Imperial Struggle for North America, 1607–1755* (Westport, CT:
    Praeger, 2000)
Phillips, George Harwood: *The Enduring Struggle: Indians in California
    History* (San Francisco: Boyd & Fraser, 1981)
Ruby, Robert H. and John A. Brown: *Indians of the Pacific Northwest:
    A History* (Norman: University of Oklahoma Press, 1981)
Sturtevant, William C., general editor: *Handbook of North American
    Indians* (Washington D.C.: Smithsonian Institution, 1978-2004)
Thornton, Russell: *American Indian Holocaust and Survival: A
    Population History Since 1492* (Norman: University of Oklahoma
    Press, 1987)
Turner, Geoffrey: *Indians of North America* (New York: Sterling Pub.
    Co., 1992)

PICTURE CREDITS

A vast majority of the photographs, lithographs, sketches, and printed ephemera in this work have been taken from the collections of the National Archives and Records Administration, the National Museum of American Indian, Smithsonian Institution and Library of Congress. The items are listed by page number and position (t-top, m-middle, b-bottom, l-left, c-centre, r-right.)

The National Archives and Records Administration Collections:
20(bl), photo no. 106-IN-18A; 21(bc), photo no. 75-ID-118A; 25(bl), 79G Box 1, Folder Q, Dept. of the Interior; 25(br), 79G Box 1, Folder G. Dept. of the Interior; 26(t), 106-FAA-54; 35(tr), 79G Box 3, Dept of the Interior; 39(tl), 79G Box 29, Folder N, Dept. of the Interior; 39(cl), 79G Box 29, Folder P, Dept. of the Interior; 39(r), 79G Box 29, Folder N, Dept. of the Interior; 43(tr), artwork no. 111-SC-83156; 44(cr), 208-LU-251-7; 46-47, 111-111-234; 50(tr), photo no. 75-N-SEM-47; 65(tl), photo no. 111-SC-103716; 74-75, 111-111-234; 79(cl), photo no. 106-IN-78; 79(tr), artwork no. 111-SC-92844; 81(bl), photo no. 111-SC-82493; 81(tl), artwork no. 111-SC-93123; 83(br), artwork no. 111-SC-97367; 87(bl), photo no. 75-IP-2-7; 86(cl), photo no. 75-IP-3-27; 91(tl), 79G Box 3, Folder P, Dept. of the Interior; 91(bl), photo no. 111-B-5272; 93(br), photo no. not available; 97(b), photo no. 111-B-4628; 99(bc), photo no. 79-HP-6-3200; 100(br), photo no. 111-SC-95986; 101(tl), photo no. 111-SC-85728; 103(l&r), photo no. 111-111-234; 105(tr), photo no. 111-SC-87772; 106(bl), photo no. 111-SC-87722; 107(bl), photo no. 111-SC-82320; 109(br), photo no. 111-SC-82320; 109(tl), photo. no. 111-SC-85775; 110(bl), photo. no. 111-AGD-73; 111(tl), photo no. 111-SC-96033; 112(tr), photo no. 111-SC-103706; 113(br), photo no. 126-ARA-2-231; 115(cr), photo no. 75-BAE-2421B-6; 115(br), photo no. 75-N-29, Folder P; 123(tl), photo no. 75-N-38, Folder T; 123(br), photo no. 75-IP-3-7; 124(cr), photo no. 79G Box 29, Folder M. Dept. of the Interior; 124(tl), photo no. 75-N-35, Folder S; 126(l), photo no. 75-N-PIM-33; 126(mc), photo no. 208-NS-4350-2; 127(br), photo no. 80-G-413988; 128(tr), photo no. 208-N-24772; 129(mc-right), photo no. 208-N-24772; 129(mc-left), photo no. 111-SC-48488; 129(tl), photo no. 127-MN-57875; 130-131, photo no. 111-111-234; 133(br), photo no. 75-N-NEW-52; 135(tr), photo no. 75-N-32, Folder R; 136(bl), photo no. 75-N-OS-51.

The Library of Congress:
2, 4, 17(tl), 24(bl), 29(tl), 31(bl), 36(br), 38, 40(tl), 44(bl), 48(cl), 48(c), 49, 50(bl), 52(t), 52(bl), 53(tr), 53(bl), 54, 55(tl), 55(tr), 56, 64(bl), 64(br), 65(tr), 66(tl), 67(tl), 68, 69, 70(br), 71(b), 72(l), 76(bl), 77(br), 81(cl), 82(tl), 83(tr), 83(cr), 84, 85, 87(br), 89(tl), 91(tr), 93(mc), 95, 102, 105(cl), 107(cl), 109(cl), 111(bl), 112(tl), 113(cr), 115(tl), 122(bl), 137(tr), 138(tl).

National Museum of the American Indian, Smithsonian Institution:
3, neg. no. 39485; photographed by the NMAI Photo Services Staff; 12(bl), 196411.000; 14(cr), 219181.000; 14(bl), neg. no. 38591; 15(cr), 250133.000; 17(b), slide no. S 6034 A-B; 35(br), P18362; 35(tl), 203569.000; 36(tr), slide no. S 5792; 41(l), 265126.000; 45(br), 250129.000; 51(cl), 180327.000; 51(bl), neg.no. 11607; 66(bl), 004722.000; 72(r), 241965.000; 79(mc), 198120.000; 88(tl), photo no. 165-MM-1623; 88(tr), photo no. 57-PE-110; 100(mc), neg.no. 30768-69; 104(bl), neg. no. 20656; 105(bl), neg. no. 26168-69, 109(mc), neg. no. 38382; 116- 117, photo no. 111-111-234; 141(tr), 265294.000; 153(b), neg. no. 39485; photographed by the NMAI Photo Services Staff.

Images from other sources:
6(tr), Indiana Historical Society, Bodmer Collection: neg. 48; 6(bl), Frisco Native American Museum, North Carolina; 8, Courtesy of the New York State Museum; 9(mc), Courtesy of the Florida Museum of Natural History "Tusks" exhibit; 9(bl), Courtesy of the Friends of Calico, photo by Chris Vedborg; 9(tl-middle & lower), Courtesy of the Pocono Indian Museum; 9(tl-upper), SBCM-1500A-2253; 10(t), Original illustration by Andrew Wilson, © 2007 Jay Wertz & Associates; 11(tl), A637-412#32, Courtesy of the San Bernardino County Museum; 11(bl), Frisco Native American Museum, North Carolina; 11(br), Courtesy of the Florida Museum of Natural History "Tusks" exhibit; 12(cl), Mask © Canadian Museum of Civilisation QkHn-13:489, photo by Ross Taylor, S90-4013; 13(bl), Courtesy of the Autry National Center Southwest Museum, Los Angeles. Photo no. 96.158.1; 14(br), Frisco Native American Museum, North Carolina; 15(t), With permission of the Royal Ontario Museum © ROM; 15(bl), Effigy Mounds National Monument, National Park Service; 16(bl) Indiana Historical Society, PO130_BOX48_FOLDER2_204897-F; 18-19 & 20(tl), Mashantucket Pequot Museum and Research Center, Archives and Special Collections; 21(tl), Courtesy of the Abbe Museum, Bar Harbor, Maine, photo by Stephen Bicknell; 21(cl), Courtesy of the New York State Museum; 21(tr), author's private collection; 22-23, Courtesy of Massachusetts Archives; 25(tr), Indiana Historical Society, Bodmer Collection: neg. #32; 26(cl), Image Courtesy of Cline Library, Northern Arizona University; 27(tl) & 27(r), Casa Grande Ruins National Monument, National Park Service, photographed by Jay Wertz; 27(cl), Gila Cliff Dwelling National Monument, National Park Service; 28(bl), Mashantucket Pequot Museum and Research Center, Archives and Special Collections; 29(bl), author's private collection; 30(t), The Historical Society of Pennsylvania; 30(br), author's private collection; 31(t), Library and Archives Canada, accession #2222222; 31(br), Frisco Native American Museum, North Carolina; 32, Courtesy of the New York State Archives and Records Administration, Albany, NY; 33, Courtesy of the Historical Society of Delaware; 34(b), NA3945; 36(bl), NA4170, 37(tl), NA832, all from University of Washington Libraries, Special Collections; 37(b), With permission of the Royal Ontario Museum © ROM; 40(tl), Navajo blanket Courtesy of the Autry National Center, Souwest Museum, Los Angeles. Photo by Schenck and Schenck no. 535.G.627; 42 & 43(br), Oklahoma Historical Society; 43(cl), Frisco Native American Museum, North Carolina; 44(tr & br), Oklahoma Historical Society; 45(l), The American Antiquarian Society; 51(cr), Fort Caroline National Memorial, National Park Service; 51(tl), The Historic New Orleans Collection; 55(tc), Frisco Native American Museum, North Carolina; 55(br), Courtesy of the Pocono Indian Museum; 57, The Historical Society of Pennsylvania; 58(mr), P.351, 58(tl), P.1366, 59(cr), LS.2868, 59(br), P.18446, all Courtesy of the Autry National Center, Southwest Museum, Los Angeles.; 61(tl), Bureau of Land Management, photo by Christopher Ross; 60(tl), Courtesy of the Autry National Center, Southwest Museum, Los Angeles. Photo no. P1048; 60(cr), Chumash Cultural Center; 61(b), Semler Family Ranch, photo by Jay Wertz; 62-63, Karpeles Manuscript Library; 67(b), NA3942, University of Washington Libraries, Special Collections; 70(mc), Indiana Historical Society, James O. Lewis Collection: plate no. 12; 71(tl), The Ohio Historical Society; 73(br), Indiana Historical Society, PO391_Box13_Vincennes; 73(tl), Indianna Historical Society, James O. Lewis Collection: plate no. 50; 77(bl), Indianna Historical Society, Bodmer Collection: neg#48; 77(tl), Wind Cave National Park, National Park Service; 78(bl), Denver Public Library, Western History Collection. Sacajawea #X33784, 78(tl), James O. Lewis Collection: plate no. 78, 78(tr), James O. Lewis Collection: plate no. 76, 79(tr), Bodmer Collection:

neg. #060, all Indiana Historical Society; 80(bl), Bodmer Collection: neg. #42, 81(mc), James O. Lewis Collection: plate no. 75, both, Indiana Historical Society; 83(bl), Mashantucket Pequot Museum and Research Center, Archives & Special Collections; 87(tc), Nevada Historical Society; 89(tr), 66.G.152, 89(bl), P.37816, both Courtesy of the Autry National Center, Southwest Museum, Los Angeles.; 90(cr), Indiana Historical Society, James O. Lewis Collection: plate no. 75; 90(bl), Pea Ridge National Military Park, National Park Service; 92(tr), Indiana Historical Society, PO406_272, created by Ferdinand Delannoy; 93(cl), Image, Courtesy Colorado Historical Society, Black Kettle F4911/10025493; 94, Letter from Black Kettle, Sand Creek Papers, Mf 0018, Colorado College Special Collections, Colorado Springs, Colorado; 96(br), The Historic New Orleans Collection; 96(bl), Oklahoma Historical Society; 97(tl), Indiana Historical Society, Bodmer Collection: neg. #5339; 98(bl), Meusebach-Comanche Indian Treaty, March 2, 1847, by Lucy Meusebach Marshall, Courtesy Gillespie County Historical Society, Fredericksburg, Texas; 98(tl), Texas State Library and Archives Commission; 99(bl), Museum of History & Industry Seattle; 107(tl), Cochise 1872 William S. Sutton © Charles Parker; 108(t), from Bureau of American Ethnology Seventeenth Annual Report; 111(tr), Alaska State Library; 111(mc), With permission of the Royal Ontario Museum © ROM; 113(tl), Anchorage Museum of History & Art; 114(bl), 115(cl), U.S. Army Heritage and Education Center, U.S. Army Military History Institute; 118(c), Courtesy of the Autry National Center, Southwest Museum, Los Angeles. photo no. P.972; 118(bl), Library and Archives Canada, accession #333333; 119(br), With permission of the Royal Ontario Museum © ROM; 119(tl), Courtesy of the New York State Museum and Archives; 119(bl), Courtesy of the Autry National Center, Southwest Museum, Los Angeles. (photo no. 96.32.3);120, 121(l&r), Karpeles Manuscript Library; 123(cr), Courtesy of the Autry National Center, Southwest Museum, Los Angeles. Photo no. P.1904; 124(tr), Courtesy of Cline Library, Northern Arizona University; 127(tl), Oklahoma Historical Society; 128(b), Image Courtesy of Cline Library, Northern Arzona University; 129(cr), Oklahoma Historical Society; 132(c), 133(tl), 134(tl), Kanien 'kehaka Onkwawén:na Raotitiohkwa Quebec; 134(bl), Adam Fortunate Eagle; 134(tc), Nevada Historical Society;135(tl), 135(cl), © Ilka Hartman, 2007; 137(tc), photograph by Maurice Seymour, Courtesy of Raymond Seymour; 138(r), Getty Images / George Pimentel; 139(tr), Courtesy of the National Hockey League and Topps Trading Card Co.; 139(cb), Courtesy of New York Yankees and Topps Trading Card Co.; 139(tc), Waneek Horn – Miller; 139(br), Office of the U.S. Senate Historian; 140(bl), Courtesy of the Wheelwright Museum of the American Indian, Santa Fe, photograph by Addison Doty; 141(cl), Buffalo Bill Historical Center; 141(br) Courtesy of the City of Poway, California; 142(bl), Adam Fortunate Eagle; 142(br), Johnny Bear Contreras; 143(tc), Courtesy of America Meredith; 143(tl), Golden Gate National Recreation Area, National Park Service; 143(br), Rob Casey Photography; 144(mb), 144(cl), 145(cr), Photographed by Jay Wertz; 145(tl), 145(bl), © Ilka Hartman, 2007; 146(bl), Copyright © of the Academy of Motion Arts & Sciences and used with permission; 147(tl), 147(bl), 147(br), Photographed by Jay Wertz; 148-151, Nevada Historical Society; 152(bl) Agua Caliente Band of Mission Indians from the collection of Johnny Bear Contreras; 153(t), Chumash Cultural Center, photo by Jay Wertz; 154(tl), Private Collection; 154(tr), Hubbell Trading Post National Historic Site, National Park Service; 154(mr-upper), Frisco Native American Museum, Frisco, North Carolina; 154 (mr-lower), Chumash Cultural Center, photo by Jay Wertz; 155(tl) Frisco Native American Museum, Frisco, North Carolina; 155(b), Image Courtesy of Cline Library, Northern Arizona University.